MAKING MONEY
WITH YOUR
CREATIVE PAINT FINISHES

LYNETTE HARRIS

NORTH LIGHT BOOKS
CINCINNATI, OHIO

This book is dedicated to Matthew and Lauren, my personal cheering section; and to Myron and Lucille, for their love and support way beyond the call of duty.

Making Money With Your Creative Paint Finishes. Copyright © 1998 by Lynette Harris. Manufactured in the United States of America. All rights reserved. No part of this book may be reproduced in any form or by any electronic or mechanical means including information storage and retrieval systems without permission in writing from the publisher, except by a reviewer, who may quote brief passages in a review. Published by North Light Books, an imprint of F&W Publications, Inc., 1507 Dana Avenue, Cincinnati, Ohio 45207. (800) 289-0963. First edition.

Other fine North Light Books are available from your local bookstore, art supply store or direct from the publisher.

02 01 00 99 98   5 4 3 2 1

Library of Congress Cataloging-in-Publication Data

Harris, Lynette
    Making money with your creative paint finishes / by Lynette Harris.—1st ed.
      p.   cm.
   Includes bibliographical references and index.
   ISBN 0-89134-824-7 (pbk. : alk. paper)
    1. House painting. 2. Furniture painting. 3. Decoration and ornament. 4. Small business. 5. Home-based businesses. I. Title.
TT323.H33 1998
745.7'23—dc21   98-19910
                                                  CIP

Content edited by David Borcherding
Production edited by Bob Beckstead
Designed by Brian Roeth
Cover photography by Pamela Monfort Braun, Bronze Photography

Acknowledgments

My deepest appreciation and gratitude to my friends for life and soul mates—my fellow decorative artists of the Stencil Artisan's League, Inc., to whom I owe a huge debt of gratitude for the inspiration, camaraderie and life support they provide.

A special thank-you to John Catalanotto, Peggy Eisenberg, Mary Jane Fisher, Deb Metler, P.J. Tetrault, Linda Radziminski, Kate Scott, Carole Haines Shearer, Claudia Stahl and Barbara Wagner.

Table of Contents

Preface

A Labor of Love

Most of the decorative painters I know have chosen this particular path because they have fallen in love with their hobby or craft. The very first time I began to stencil a wall, it was as if the heavens opened, angels sang "Hallelujah!" and trumpets blasted. It was love at first brushstroke! I *finally* knew exactly what it was I wanted to do when I became a grown-up—never mind I was already pushing thirty!

I am often asked how I got started painting. My answer always amazes people: "I have no idea." I wasn't the artistic child of the family; that was my brother's place. I didn't study art in school, nor did I study design. I didn't apprentice with anyone. Heck, I couldn't draw much more than stick figures. But even as a child, nothing thrilled me more than color. Color is my passion. To this day, a new box of crayons quickens my pulse and lights a fire in my soul! But, believing I was not an artist, I chose a different path, becoming a legal secretary, a wife and a mother.

During the mid-1980s, I found myself thoroughly bored with my part-time secretarial job and realized I needed a new job, something that would better fit my needs: flexible hours (I had two small children) and good pay, but, most importantly, something that fed my soul, which typing and filing definitely did not. When my son came down with the chicken pox, and my boss did not want me to stay home with him, it was the final straw. I quit.

Remember, this was the mid-1980s and country-style decorating was all the rage. I wanted a simple stenciled border painted in my family room, but couldn't find anyone to hire to paint it for me. So I mentally shrugged and said, "How hard can this be?" Using a very wet stencil brush (after all, I wet the brushes in my beginner's tole-painting class), I applied craft paint to the brush and rubbed it through a thick quilt stencil onto the semigloss-painted wall. I am amazed it even stayed on the wall, and yet, I fell in love! I, the nonartistic child of my family, could paint! It spoke to me, loud and clear: "This is what you have been looking for all along!"

I went to my local library and checked out every book I could find on stenciling and decorative painting. There weren't many, but I hungrily devoured them. I stenciled my own house, my friends' homes and my parents' home. It almost became a joke: If it wasn't moving, look out! I'd stencil it! This was quickly becoming addictive, and I knew there was no turning back. However, I needed to justify the time, energy and money I was investing in this love affair—so, with very little experience under my belt, I placed a small advertisement in the local paper: "Custom Decorative Stenciling, call Lynette." With more nerve than sense, my decorative painting career was launched.

During the past twelve years, I have built three very different decorative painting businesses. My first business, "Stencils With Style," was strictly stenciling. I painted miles and miles of stenciled borders complete with ducks and pineapples. As the country look began to evolve into a more sophisticated decorating style, so did the stenciling industry. A more artistic, painterly approach to stenciling demanded that stencil designs become more free-form, more lifelike and, consequently, more complicated. As my business became more and more successful, I began to feel harried and overbooked, because I wasn't able to keep up with the demand. Finally, I called a woman I had taken classes from earlier and asked if she would be willing to work for me until this busy time passed. With a little arm twisting, she agreed to try it for a while. We found that we worked very well together; our personalities and painting styles meshed perfectly. Her talents brought a new direction to my business, and we decided to form a partnership. This was how my second decorative painting business, "Illusions of Grandeur," was born. We began to experiment with glazed wall finishes, faux finishes and murals, both freehand and stenciled. Our skills and personalities complemented each other, and our business took off. Sadly, at this time my husband was offered a better job, and we decided to relocate our family from Southern California to Chicago. I had to leave my business in midstride, after I had worked so hard to nurture it. This was a very difficult, but necessary, decision.

It was a good move for our family. After everyone was settled, I realized I hungered to get back to work. I blithely assumed I could reestablish my decorative painting business anywhere with very little effort. After all, I already knew how to paint, and had my portfolio to prove it. I had tons of experience with marketing. I felt I knew exactly what to do. But did I get humbled in a hurry! It was a surprisingly difficult struggle, as I was little prepared for how emotionally devastating it would be for me to face rejection, to reinvent my business and myself, to repay my dues yet another time and sell myself all over again. It was this test of my enthusiasm, dedication and spirit that truly taught me about being an artist. However, it was the demise of my marriage, and with that a reassessment of my financial needs, that taught me about being a professional, a true businesswoman. If I was going to continue in my labor of love, I would have to build my business to such a level that I could support myself and my children. To quote my mother, "Desperation is the mother of all creativity." And I desperately wanted to continue painting.

The wisdom and experience I gained in the process are the premise for this book. I will share what I've learned, either by dumb luck (preferably called "happy accidents") or free-falling down the learning curve (trial and error). I will share my own personal experiences, as well as tips and advice from other decorative painters, to provide a safety net for you as you leap from hobbyist to professional.

"Optimism is the faith that leads to achievement."

—HELEN KELLER

Introduction

Making the Leap From Hobbyist to Professional

A decorative painting business stands apart from other small businesses. While the business philosophies that make any business successful still ring true, becoming a professional decorative painter often requires you to be creative on demand. The extra challenge of allowing your artistic spirit its true, creative voice, while still managing to juggle the minutiae of the business-oriented details, makes for a profession that will rarely, if ever, be dull and monotonous.

The most important elements for establishing a successful decorative painting business are enthusiasm, conviction, nerve, energy and dedication. These are essential to success. Skills can be learned and talent can be acquired—but without enthusiasm, few ventures can succeed, especially a business based on a labor of love, such as decorative painting.

So, you've been dabbling with paint for years or perhaps, like me, you have discovered the joy of painting for the first time. Your home showcases your talents and your love for your craft. Friends and family have asked you to paint in their homes. You love doing the work, but lately there's been a marked dissatisfaction in working away with no remuneration. Or perhaps you find you need to earn an income to support your habit. You say to yourself, "Hey, if I'm going to keep painting for everyone, perhaps I ought to consider doing this professionally!" But then the doubt creeps in: "How can I find the time? How can I invest in a new business when we're barely making ends meet? How can I juggle home and family? How can I do this? Don't all artists starve?" But you just know this is something you would love to be doing. "Can I make this work?" And with firm resolve, you decide to look at this folly as something more—an opportunity, perhaps, an avenue of self-expression. Your niche, so to speak. So now what?

Does the distinction between a hobbyist and a professional come from earning money with your craft? Or does professional status come from an acquired skill level that separates an amateur from a pro? I believe the answer to both questions is yes. Anyone who makes the commitment can become a professional decorative painter. Anyone with the desire, enthusiasm, energy and dedication to lay the essential foundation.

There are many reasons for wanting to start a decorative painting business, and your reason will be highly personal, as will your goals and desires for your business. Some artists want to earn enough money to support their love for their craft; others want to add a second income to the family pot; some may want little monetary reward, but seek social recognition and public accolades; still others want to earn enough money to support a staff and an army of employees. While the measure of success may be different for each of these scenarios, all of these business goals are valid, and each requires the same building blocks: acquiring necessary skills, forming a business plan, setting goals and marketing the business, plus maintaining a healthy dose of dedication and courage.

A Sketch of This Book

In the first chapter of this book I will focus on the many steps necessary for laying a solid business foundation, such as naming your business and how to acquire the basic skills necessary to be a top-notch decorative painter. This chapter also helps you define your hopes and dreams for your business by formulating a coherent plan that will provide a road map to guide you along the path to success in simple, easy-to-follow steps.

Legal and financial management are aspects of the business most artists wish would just go away, but the second chapter will painlessly provide you with the necessary tools for setting up a business: opening appropriate bank accounts, filing required business documents, obtaining insurance and keeping the IRS happy (because if the IRS isn't happy, believe me, no one's happy!).

The third chapter, on business management, will help you carve out your own office space and give you tips for dealing with home-based businesses. This chapter will help you design your work space, whether you chose to set aside an entire room for an artist studio, use a portion of the garage or simply lay claim to the dining room table, and explores unique filing systems to help keep you organized and provide you with a life preserver to save you from drowning in a sea of paperwork. Suggestions for time management are also covered in this chapter.

The section of the third chapter dedicated to supplies and equipment spells out the rudimentary supplies and the tools of the trade you will need when starting your business. This chapter includes a master supply list, which can be copied and placed in your work area, that provides you with a helpful "shopping list" as supplies need to be replenished or serves as a checklist or reminder of the equipment to be loaded into your work vehicle to take to the job site.

Chapter four pinpoints the most important step for your business— marketing. Without marketing you will have no business. Marketing focuses on getting your name known and your work "out there." The development of a showstopping portfolio and careful attention to printed materials, like business cards, fliers and brochures, as well as other marketing tools such as advertising strategies and networking ideas, are examined at length. This chapter will help you find a marketing style that suits your personality and your business philosophy.

Chapter five walks you through the minefields of determining fair and competitive pricing for your work and preparing the client's estimate. Answering the questions in the checklist will help you determine your pricing structure. The simple mathematical equations help even the most mathematically challenged (like me!) determine billing rates.

Chapter six prepares you for the initial client appointment by helping you prepare a professional-quality presentation to woo prospective clientele. Although client relations are the backbone of the decorative painting business, this chapter will also provide you with tips to "cut to the chase" in order to keep this presentation on track.

The most intensive chapter of the book, "Proposals, Contracts and Letters of Agreement," is sadly a sign of our times. Putting it in writing and spelling out the rights and responsibilities of all the parties involved can help alleviate endless grief should problems arise. This chapter will help you determine the method of contracting that works best for your business application.

Chapter eight is devoted to the art of sample making. The painted sample is another tool, albeit a more colorful and visual tool than a contract, to provide the decorative painter and the client with a means of communicating their expectations. Various sample-making tips and products are covered.

Chapter nine, "Managing the Job Site," zeroes in on the actual workaday painting situation, with a simple step-by-step approach to making your painting day more efficient, organized, productive and pleasurable.

Chapter ten focuses on industry relations with other professionals with whom a decorative painter needs to develop a rapport, such as interior designers, contractors and subcontractors. Learning how to develop a mutually respectful working relationship is the key to success, and this chapter delves into making those all-important contacts, handling referral fees and practicing business ethics.

Chapter eleven spotlights the issue of partnerships and employees, addressing the benefits of sharing the workload with another person, physically and emotionally. The mechanics of partnership agreements, hiring agreements and well-defined job descriptions are some of the finer points discussed.

Chapter twelve is entitled "Craftsmanship." The dictionary defines a *craftsman* as an artisan who creates or performs with dexterity. The chapter provides a not-so-subtle reminder of all the clichés your mother told you, from "neatness counts" to "do your best," all of which will help you become a master craftsman and a master decorative painter.

Your biggest business asset is you! Thus, the final chapter is devoted to taking care of this valuable asset, with tips on relieving overstressed muscles, avoiding burnout, and keeping the love affair with painting alive.

The book concludes with an Appendix of useful business forms, a recommended reading list and resource lists of product suppliers and schools for learning decorative painting skills.

Chapter 1

Laying the Foundation for Your Business

S tarting your decorative business with a good, solid foundation will be instrumental to your success. To me, training and education rank highest in importance when it comes to preparing your foundation, for without learning the necessary skills, there will be little substance to your business. I rank planning and forethought, which means developing a business plan, second. A business plan is the road map you will need to achieve success. But the best place to begin is by naming the "baby." Giving a name to your decorative painting business will help to ground the perhaps nebulous concept that is bouncing around in your head.

Naming the Business

There are several directions you can take when coming up with a name for your business. Consider names relating to your locality; i.e., a name based on something in the area in which you will be working. My business, North Shore Wall Design, was named for the suburbs north of Chicago where I currently live. Another example, Beartooth Designs, is the name of Candie Duren's business because she lives in view of the Beartooth mountain ranges of Montana.

You could choose a business name which simply states the service your business intends to offer, such as Carole Haines Shearer's business, Stenciling, Etc., or Donna Evans's business, Artistic Custom Stenciling.

Another type of business name is related to name recognition for you as the artist, such as Mary Jane Fisher Decorative Painting or Claudia's Climbing the Walls. Using your name in conjunction with your business is a good way to ensure people remember both your name *and* your business name.

And of course, some business names are simply fun and creative, like Christina Gibson's Elegant Whimsey or Sheri Hoeger's The Mad Stencilist, which is what her son called her.

Spend some time on this naming process: You will not want to be stuck with a name that doesn't fit you, or one that could be misinterpreted as offering services not at all related to your business. When you have come up with a name you are happy with, you will have to do a business-name search in conjunction with your secretary of state's office or state business licensing board to be sure that no other business is currently using that name.

Fine Tuning Your Decorative Painting Skills

Absorb all the knowledge you can about painting techniques and art fundamentals, because knowledge and experience will be key ingredients in your business foundation.

As a decorative painter, you will always be on a learning curve. No matter how many times you've painted any given finish, it will never be the same application twice. Each job will present new challenges. Problem-solving is really what it's all about. You can enhance the odds of solving the problem correctly by fine tuning your skills with practice and experience—either your own or someone else's experience—and by being willing to continue to learn.

Every time you pick up a paintbrush, it becomes a learning experience. Regardless of how many years of experience you have under your belt, you can always learn something new. Once you stop trying new techniques or stretching your skill level a little higher, you will become stagnant and stale. The best way to avoid falling into a predictable rut is to push yourself into learning new techniques and working with new products or in a different medium. Never be afraid to become a beginner again!

No matter whether you've been self-taught (like I have) or have studied art formally, there are certain prerequisite skills necessary to running a decorative painting business.

• *Learn fundamental art skills* and have a rudimentary understanding of the basics of painting: color theory, perspective, balance (scale and proportion), simple brushstrokes, stencil design and cutting, and various properties and workings of paint and glaze mediums, as well as the uses of the various tools and brushes available to the decorative painter. The basic principles of painting must be learned before weak points can be strengthened and strengths can be carried to master-quality level through review and continued practice. Most community colleges, continuing-education facilities and art schools teach these subjects.

There are schools (see Appendix C) that also specialize in teaching more advanced decorative painting techniques. Although most of these schools are expensive, this investment will add new dimension to your business and to you as an artist. Studying at one of the renowned schools also adds credibility to your ever-growing resume.

But if one of these intensive seminars is not within your budget, check with your local community college, craft store or art guild, as these establishments also offer classes in decorative painting techniques. If you are just starting out, try to take as many classes as possible. If you are fairly well established, strive to take at least one class a year, even if the class

"Painting is easy when you don't know how, but very difficult when you do."

—EDGAR DEGAS

offered is technique you feel you already know. Many times I have taken a class on a certain technique, but came away with other useful tidbits, such as handy work tips or shortcuts, not only from the teacher, but from other students as well. Budget and invest the time and money necessary to strengthen your decorative skills.

Investing time and energy in classes will both strengthen you as an artist and allow you to bring more confidence to your business.

• *Read* everything you can get your hands on about decorative painting. Many books are available on faux finishing, stenciling and decorative painting. All of these books offer different insights into painting techniques and procedures. Study, take notes and experiment. I strongly suggest developing a good research library so you can have books at hand to use for references when a painting challenge arises. Subscribe to decorative painting magazines and magazines showing the latest decorating trends. Magazine articles are a great way to keep up with new products and techniques, as well as market trends. (See Appendix A for a recommended reading list of books and magazines you will want to check out.)

• *Practice* your craft. Just as a musician must practice scales and exercises, the decorative painter must practice the basics. Practice by painting sample boards, by exploring different brushstrokes, by experimenting with various stenciling methods or by sketching something in proper perspective. Practice color theory by getting some primary paints and mixing colors. Color theory is fun when you "play" with the colors! Practicing these techniques will improve your dexterity and skill.

Use the surfaces of your own home as your learning boards—try different techniques on the walls and furniture. Practice painting techniques on garage sale and flea market finds or on old furniture that you can use for a palette. Experiment, practice and sample. Try different techniques.

"When people ask me, 'How'd you learn to do this?' my famous answer is to say, 'If you spend the time and read a book, you can do anything.' "

—SHARON GARIZIO

Try different methods. Compare different products. Take notes and keep records of what works best under which conditions. Be sure to write everything down. At the time you think you will never forget how you achieved that result, but often before you can close the paint lid, the procedures start to get fuzzy and begin to escape you. Make copious notes and keep them filed in a binder for later reference.

• *Keep abreast of new products* as they become available. The painting industry is evolving at lightning speed to keep up with the demands of the decorating market. Be sure the staff at your local paint store and artist supply store understand enough about your business to keep you updated. The Internet is a great way to keep on top of the market. (See Appendix B for a list of Internet resources.)

• *Establish a clip file* folder just for inspiration: Fill it with anything that sparks your imagination. Mine includes greeting cards, pages from old calendars, magazine pictures, catalog backdrops, color copies from library books and pages of garden catalogs. Clip articles and photographs that show decorative painting. Also clip articles about painting techniques.

Over the years my "idea file" has grown so large that I had to divide it up into smaller files, such as furniture painting, mural ideas, stenciling and painting techniques.

• *Apprentice yourself* by offering your services to an established decorative painter, if you are lucky enough to have one in your area. Give the pro a reason to hire you. Present a well-written letter of introduction, a resume and some photographs of your painted work. There is no better way to learn the ropes of the business than by joining up with someone willing to teach you. I have found that most decorative painters are willing to share their knowledge and love of their craft when the apprentice shares the same enthusiasm.

• *Join painting organizations* so you can network with other artists and decorative painters. This is another way to continue to grow and educate yourself. As most of this business is trial and error, learn from the successes and mistakes of others. Never be afraid to ask for help.

There are several networking organizations dedicated to promoting decorative painting (see Appendix B). The Stencil Artisan's League, Inc. (SALI) is an educational organization that promotes stenciling and all the related arts. SALI has many local chapters around the country, including a chapter that corresponds on the Internet. SALI hosts a convention each summer with classes taught by the best of the best and a trade show filled with every decorative painting product imaginable. Attending a SALI convention is a magical experience. You will be surrounded by decorative painters of all ability levels—and can learn from each of them.

There is something energizing about being among people who share your love for decorative painting, people who speak the same language and who understand your mission. This is the biggest benefit of joining decorative painting groups.

Creating a Business Plan

Most decorative painters, being the right-brained creatures we are, have a hard time putting sound business practices (left-brained exercises) into use. Preparing a business plan is indeed a sound practice. Unfortunately, the idea of creating a business plan brings forth images of corporate strategy, charts, graphs and spreadsheets. But this exercise needn't be complicated: A business plan is simply a written tool allowing you to focus on your needs, hopes and dreams for your business. Establishing a business plan forces you to stop and think, to plan and to validate your business agenda rather than simply allowing yourself to be buffeted around by forces beyond your control. It need not be a lengthy document—however, it should be in writing. The very act of putting words on paper forces you to assess just what it *is* you're trying to accomplish. Your business plan should include the following elements.

1. Purpose Statement

The first part of a good business plan is a clear and succinct statement of what your business is. The corporate world calls this a ''mission, or purpose, statement." For example, consider this statement by Kate Scott of Art & Accents:

The purpose of this business is the creation of useful and decorative items (functional art) for home, garden and personal use.

2. Market

Next you need to identify the market for your business. If you are a decorative painter who wants to specialize in painting children's murals, the market will be different than the market for a decorative painter who specializes in faux finishes, and still different than that of the decorative painter who specializes in marketing custom-painted floorcloths. Evaluate all avenues for marketing your new business or, if you are already established, for finding new marketing areas to branch out into. For example, "I want to send letters of introduction to all the interior designers in my area." Or, "I will market my floorcloths in the antique store on South Street." In your business plan, try to list ten new areas in which to market your business within the next year. You may want to include an area you have already begun to market your business in, but where you wish to redouble your efforts. Don't be afraid to include at least one "stretch," or one "dream market," as your goal. (Marketing ideas are discussed at length in chapter four.)

3. Establishing Margin

For all I understood of the concept, the word *margin* might as well have been written in Greek. Loosely defined, margin means keeping track of your bottom line—profit and expenses. In this part of your business plan, you will succinctly state your track record of profit and expenses. Are you working in the black or in the red? What can you do to bring your

---

"All businesses should have a business plan, even something as simple as writing down ten goals and the steps to achieve them. Post it on the wall so you can see it often. We need to focus instead of just letting each job unfold."

—SHARON A. MARRIOTT

business into the black, if you are functioning in the red? If you are just starting out and do not have a lot of (or any) data to draw upon to define your margin, simply make a statement to use this year to determine your margin by keeping accurate records of time and materials, establishing your pricing structure and stating your bookkeeping methods, which are essential to growing a healthy business. Another simple question to answer in this section of your business plan: Are you working smarter, not harder? What steps can you take to ensure that you are indeed working smarter? (See Appendix A for a list of business books that will give you more advice on establishing a margin.)

4. Advertising

Planning your advertising strategy is important to growing your business: You won't have much of a business if no one knows about you. Make a list of all advertising sources available to you, and decide which ones will target your market most effectively. Advertising is expensive, so take the time to plan, budget and evaluate which means of advertising will be most cost-effective for your business. Don't forget to include networking opportunities, as networking usually requires less cash investment, but more of a time investment by you. (Advertising and networking strategies are discussed in chapter four.) After reviewing all your options, state which contacts you want to make over the next year, and list at least one printed advertising goal and five networking goals on your business plan.

5. Educational Goals

Continuing to fine tune your skills is important to avoid stagnation and burnout, so always include educational goals in your business plan. Try to add a new skill or a new technique, or to use a different medium, as often as possible. Don't forget to include one class taken just for the fun of it. Another educational goal could be something not related to painting at all, but beneficial to your business, such as improving your computer skills, because all businesses will require some computer knowledge eventually. In your business plan, list five educational goals for you as a decorative painter, one educational goal just for fun and one business-oriented educational goal.

6. Financial Goals

Set realistic goals, but don't be afraid to reach for the moon. If it's your first year in business, how much money do you think you can earn in one year? How much do you *need* to earn in one year? Do you need a business loan?

If you've already established your business, did you earn enough last year? What will happen if you adjust your prices? Can you double your income this year? Can you start a retirement account? If you need to raise your income, how will you accomplish this? Answering these and similar questions will help you understand your financial needs and expectations. List at least five financial goals for your business.

7. Business Goals

Try to set five immediate business goals (to be accomplished within the next couple weeks), five short-term business goals (to be accomplished within the next few months) and five medium-term goals (within the year). These goals might include updating your portfolio, organizing your work space, keeping better records, hiring an assistant, revising your contract, saying no to the jobs you abhor or setting definitive working hours.

8. Long-Term Goals

No business can grow without some plan for the future. Where do you see yourself next year? In three years? In ten years? List at least ten long-term goals and ten more "before I die" goals (hopefully that's called "really-long-term goals"). These goals could include specific projects, such as, "I want my work published in *Better Homes and Gardens*," or hidden desires like "I want to write a book" or "I want to have my own video series." Or, like me: "I want to earn enough money to send my son to college." How about "I want to take my brushes and travel the country doing itinerant work" or "I want to open a school and teach children how to stencil."? Let your mind wander a bit. Don't forget, these goals are yours, and they are all valid: If it makes you uncomfortable, they need not be shared with anyone—but be sure to include them in your business plan.

Taking the time to write down your business plan acknowledges your hopes and dreams, as well as spelling out your bottom-line needs for your business. Your business plan will provide you with a road map to meeting and exceeding your goals. This is a powerful exercise.

Summary

Naming your business is the first step toward acknowledging that you are in business.

1. When naming your business, you can choose a name based on
   a. Your locality
   b. What services you will offer
   c. Your name
   d. A totally unrelated, but catchy concept
2. Register your business name with your secretary of state.

A major step toward establishing yourself as a professional is to fine tune your decorative painting skills. The steps to do this include

1. Learn fundamental painting skills, such as color theory and perspective.
2. Read everything you can get your hands on.
3. Take classes and be a willing student.
4. Practice your craft.
5. Keep abreast of all decorative painting products and tools.
6. Establish an "idea" or clip file.
7. Offer to become an apprentice to an established decorative painter.
8. Join decorative painting organizations.

The simple steps for writing your business plan include

1. Establish your purpose or mission statement.
2. Identify your market.
3. Establish your margin (profit and expense).
4. Plan an advertising and networking strategy.

5. Set educational goals.

6. Set financial goals.

7. Set short-term business goals.

8. Set long-term business goals.

Don't worry if some of your goals overlap "categories"—that's actually a good thing. Be sure to post your business plan in a prominent place so you can refer to it often.

Chapter 2

Legal and Financial Management

The legal and financial management of a decorative painting business includes aspects of the business most artists wish would just "go away." But unfortunately, the rest of the world doesn't function that way, and we must learn to step up to the plate when those unpleasant business tasks loom larger than life. I've found that working within the parameters of the local licensing boards, the state tax revenue boards, the banking institutions and the Internal Revenue Service is not all that complicated or time-consuming. While each state and local agency has different laws and restrictions for small businesses, the overall foundation is the same.

I strongly advise anyone even mildly serious about starting a decorative painting business to take all the necessary steps to establish themselves legitimately as a business from the starting gate, rather than just fumbling along. This advice comes from personal experience. When I first started out, I just added my painting income to the family pot, not keeping the business income or expenses separate from the family's personal accounts. While I never did anything blatantly illegal, I now cringe at some of my earlier business practices. I certainly didn't know anything about running a small business, and I wasn't very professional. I firmly believe that you have to act like you're a big business, even if it's just you as a sole proprietorship. The amount of credibility you grant yourself as a businessperson is directly proportional to how well your business will succeed.

Managing the Business Legalities

In order to meet the legal requirements for your business, you will have to do a bit of detective work to determine exactly what the requirements are in your particular city, county and state. I suggest you start with the local agencies (City Hall), moving up to the county agencies (the County Registrar), on to the state agencies (the State Tax Board and the State Licensing Board) and wind up with the federal agencies (the IRS). All of these agencies are listed in the yellow pages, so let your fingers do the walking.

With each agency, explain that you are starting a home-based business, tell them a bit about yourself and your business and, given all that, ask the following questions:

1. What are the licensing requirements?
2. What forms do I need to file and how do I file them? What are the filing costs?
3. Is there anything else I need to know before I establish myself in business?

The Small Business Development Centers funded by the Small Business Administration and scattered throughout the country, are another helpful resource.

Doing this research is extremely important to establishing a firm foundation for your business. Having these issues resolved and questions answered before you begin earning income is a very important step in managing your business properly.

Setting Up Your "Doing Business As" Business

I assume you will establish your business as you, as an individual, doing business as an individual (sometimes called the "me, myself and I" business). You could set yourself up as a corporation, which I will discuss later in this chapter, but most decorative painters find that they do not need the added start-up costs required to incorporate. The alternative to incorporating is setting up your business as DBA business: John Doe *doing business as* XYZ Painting. This is the most common practice.

Licenses Required for a DBA Business

Your first step is to contact your local Small Business Administration offices or your local Bar Association to find out what the licensing requirements are for a home-based businesses in your particular city and state, because licensing requirements vary from city to city, even within the same local area, and every state has different requirements for small businesses. Do not assume that requirements will be the same for you as they are for your decorative painting acquaintance who lives in another county or state.

Most cities that require you to purchase a local business license do so as a citywide revenue-raising tactic, but licenses are a requirement nonetheless. My city in California required a business license; my city here in Illinois does not. I could not advertise in my local paper in California until I provided the newspaper with a copy of my business license.

Second, you will need to file a DBA ("doing business as") form with your local county Registrar. This form registers you as the owner of record and responsible party for your business. The form is filled out and filed with the county, and then published in your local paper for a set period of time. After publication, the Registrar will send you a final-version, file-stamped copy, which you will need to establish a bank account. The filing fees and publication fees of the DBA form will cost approximately $75 to $100. You will have to provide your bank with a filed copy of your DBA form to open your business bank accounts.

And finally, contact a good accountant to help you understand the requirements the State Tax Boards and IRS have for your business. An accountant can help you establish accurate record-keeping methods right off the bat, and can also alert you to deductions and write-offs for legitimate business expenses you may not be aware of.

Incorporating Your Business

The differences between running your business as an individual entity or as a corporation are many. The main difference incorporating makes is that it takes the individual out of the business, leaving the business an entity unto itself. This is helpful in a business such as ours, where the liability risk is high. The individual (meaning *you*) and personal assets would be protected from the corporation's liability. For example, if Mr. Q. Client were to sue John Doe doing business as XYZ Decorative Painting for damages that John did to Mr. Client and Mr. Client's property, John Doe would be personally liable, and all his personal property would be subjected to claims creditors. However, if XYZ Decorative Painting was established as a corporation (XYZ Decorative Painting, Inc.), John Doe's personal property would be protected from Mr. Client's claim—only the business and business assets would be liable. Therefore, being incorporated would insulate you, as an individual, from personal liability. There are some downsides to incorporation, however. Incorporation costs can be hefty to a newly founded business. While the costs vary from state to state, the average fees are usually well over $1,000. Corporations require more extensive bookkeeping and different income tax filings, as you would have to file a tax return for the corporation and a personal return for yourself. Basically, the income earned by a corporation is taxed twice: Income paid to the corporation would be taxed, and any income John Doe paid himself from the corporation would also be taxed again.

Perhaps you will want to start out as a sole proprietorship and, as your business grows, consider filing for incorporation later. You will have to determine which type of business best fits you and your specific needs.

Managing the Business Finances

Your next step will be to contact your bank and see what their requirements are for you to establish a business bank account. As I stated before, most banks will require you to provide them with a copy of your filed DBA form. Do not hesitate to shop around, as the banking industry has become very competitive, and some banks will offer you better service and rates than others.

Establish a separate credit card account for your business when you open your business accounts. Some banks have package deals where a credit card is included with the account for no extra charge. Having a business credit account is handy for placing orders for supplies by phone, or for big-ticket items you need for the business but want to pay for over a period of time—or as soon as you are paid by your customer.

Never run business funds through your personal account. Not only does this wreak havoc on your bookkeeping, but it is discouraging to see your business funds sucked up in the vortex of daily life. How can you keep track of your income if you are using that income to purchase school clothes for the children? (Not that there's anything wrong with that, but run the income through the business account first.) Deposit all income into the business account and then pay yourself a salary out of the business account to put into your personal account. This amount can fluctuate as your business grows.

Bookkeeping

Keep accurate banking records by using a separate accounting ledger book purchased at your local stationery store. Be sure to document and itemize all income and each expense. You can use one ledger sheet for the entire accounting period, or you can use one sheet per month, whichever is convenient for you and your accounting system.

In my ledger book, I prefer separate quarterly pages, making a column for each of the following expense entries (which also correlate to the business deductions I claim on my income tax return):

Paint and Painting Supplies	Labor and Referral Fees
Office Expenses	Dues and Publications
Automobile Expenses	Insurance
Advertising	Taxes
Educational Expenses	Legal and Professional Services
Travel and Entertainment	Miscellaneous

I record my income on a separate ledger page, making a notation of the client's name, the date, the job description and the billing method (i.e., Smith—labor: 400 sq. ft. wall glazing × $2/ft.) in a column allocated to "labor." In a separate column I write down any income billed separately for "materials."

There are several computer programs available to help you do your bookkeeping on computer if you are so inclined. Quicken is a good banking/bookkeeping program that is easy to use; Excel can be customized to fit your individual bookkeeping needs.

Whether you use a ledger book or a computer program, updating your accounts at regular intervals makes the bookkeeping process much easier than trying to unravel a whole year's worth of financial transactions at tax time, which is stressful enough without having to jigsaw-puzzle-piece your records together. If monthly record keeping isn't convenient, at least commit to record keeping quarterly. How can you know where you are going (financially speaking) if you don't know where you've been?

Needless to say, you will want to keep this ledger book in a safe place, and you will find it extremely helpful at tax time to have all your business deductions already neatly logged and categorized.

Keeping the IRS Happy

I strongly recommend hiring a good accountant for tax advice before you start out. Even large companies struggle with the tax issues, and because each business is different, each individual tax scenario will be different too. As you are the CEO of your company, it is up to you to educate yourself on your tax liability and the responsibilities of your business. Not knowing the rules or the laws is no excuse. If you must contact the IRS with questions, be sure to get all tax advice in writing.

My eyes glaze over whenever the tax tables come out, so perhaps you will want to do as I do and seek professional advice—but do it in the early stages of setting up your business, before too many bad habits are entrenched, and seek tax advice well before tax season. If hiring an accountant is not within your budget, consider offering to trade painting services for tax advice. Many CPAs' offices could be brightened with a little paint!

If you have established your business as an individual (doing business as) entity, you will not need a tax identification number. Your tax information will be filed and recorded under your Social Security number. You will simply file your business income and deductions on Schedule C of the Form 1040.

After your first year in business, the IRS will determine whether or not you will need to make estimated quarterly tax payments. Of course, if your business had a loss the first year (which most businesses do when they have so many start-up costs), you will not be required to make quarterly payments during the next year. There is a catch to this, however, for if your business starts earning a lot more income, the IRS expects you to make estimated quarterly payments anyway. You and your accountant will need to monitor your income and determine how much of an estimated payment you should be making to avoid any penalties.

It's a good idea to set aside anywhere between 15 to 28 percent of your gross income to cover your tax liability.

Insurance

What is it about insurance that can make my hands clammy just at the mere thought? Perhaps insurance policies force us to face all the worst-case scenarios and what-ifs. But you should never, ever consider painting even one job without liability insurance coverage. Do not risk going into someone else's home or business to apply paint without having liability insurance. There are liability insurance policies through some of the decorative painting guilds (I purchased mine through the Stencil Artisan's League), and I advise checking into this, because large groups such as these can get better rates than as individuals. I have a policy that provides a million dollars coverage with a $200 deductible. That should cover just about any nightmare I could dream up. This policy costs approximately $300 per year.

My business goal for this year is to add disability insurance to my never-ending list of insurance policies. Having had a few near-mishaps, I can no longer afford to not have it. If I am hurt or injured, which means I cannot work, my family could go hungry.

Because I do not have employees (my assistants are all subcontractors and not employees), I do not carry Workman's Compensation insurance, but this is required if you have anyone working for you. The Small Business Administration in your community can provide information on applying for Workman's Compensation insurance.

If you have a large amount of inventory, be sure your homeowner's or renter's policy covers your business assets—your inventory or your painting supplies.

Be sure the automobile you use for business is registered and insured as a business vehicle. This will cost a little more, but the coverage provides you with added protection should your vehicle do damage to a client's property, or if business assets are damaged in your vehicle.

Summary

1. Contact your local government (City Hall), your county government (Registrar's office), your state government (the Secretary of State's office, the state tax board and the state licensing board) and the

federal government (IRS) concerning the specific licensing and tax requirements for your particular business in your particular area.

2. Establish separate business checking and credit accounts.

3. Keep an accurate bookkeeping ledger and update it at least quarterly.

4. Hire a good accountant for tax advice.

5. Never consider painting any job without liability insurance.

Chapter 3

Business Management

It's not enough to be a great decorative *artiste*—you must also have the business savvy to back up your artistic talent. Learning to manage the business aspects of your decorative painting business will be vital to its success.

Operating a Home-Based Business

Running a home-based business can bring out the entrepreneurial spirit in the best of us. However, there is definitely good news *and* bad news associated with home-based businesses. The good news is that you are home during work hours; the bad news is that you are home during work hours.

The first step to maintaining control of your home-based business is to admit to yourself and your family that you are operating a *business* out of your home. Solicit their help, encouragement and support. This step is essential, because the business will impact the family unit, and the family unit will affect the business—even if that unit is you and your cat.

Second, you must establish your "office" space. Whether it's just a corner or a whole room of your very own, this space must be inviolate. Nothing is as disheartening as adding the business clutter to the family clutter and not being able to control either. Keeping both separate right from the start is imperative to maintaining order.

And finally, you will need a space to paint, to practice your techniques and to prepare sample boards, which will be your work space or studio.

My biggest problem with working at home was that there never seemed to be an end to my workday. While others could leave their office and go home, I was always surrounded by mine—returning phone calls late in the evening or painting samples in the dawn's early light. I finally figured out a solution to my never-ending workday. I discovered the telephone caused me the most problems: My solution was to install a separate phone line so I could turn on the recorder when I wasn't ''at work.'' I found it also helped to physically close the door and leave the office when done for the day. On the other side of the coin, it was easy to be distracted by home matters when I should have been working. I quickly learned that I had to leave the load of laundry until after business hours. It's very easy to assume you can handle both the home front and the business front, simply because you are working from your home, but this mentality will quickly cause even the most enthusiastic entrepreneur to feel the candle burning at both ends.

Telephone Lines

I recommend installing a separate phone line exclusively for your business phone calls. I have two teenagers, and I'm sure I would never receive a single call if we only had one phone line. Having the business line ring exclusively in your office truly delineates business calls from personal calls. But I found having a business-only telephone line was a too bit restrictive for me, as I either forgot to check the office for messages or was afraid to leave the office for fear of missing an important call. My solution was to have a cordless phone hooked up to my business line so I could carry the phone to other parts of my house, including into the studio (also known as my garage) when I was expecting an important call. But sometimes I found that having a phone in the studio was more of a distraction than I could handle. There are times when I don't want the phone to intrude, such as when I am designing or painting samples and covered with paint. The last thing I want to do is talk business with a client when my brushes are getting crispy or my hands are covered in paint. I found my phone manners were not at their best if I was interrupted while flinging paint onto sample boards. I've learned that sometimes it's best to let my answering machine pick up and take a message for me. I can return the phone call as soon as my hands are free. Take a little time to plan out how you want your telephone system installed in your business area and what phone methods work best for you.

If you want to advertise in the yellow pages, the phone line must be listed as a business line with the phone company. Business phone lines are more expensive than personal phone lines, but if you are going to write off the cost of the telephone as a business expense, that phone line should be a business line. Of course, in this day of fax machines and computer modems, we could be talking about adding a third or fourth phone line!

The important point here is to be able to establish a link to your clientele that does not interfere with your family and vice versa. Nothing is more frustrating than having a client call in the middle of dinner or early on a Sunday morning (what *are* they thinking?). And on the opposite side of the coin, it can be equally frustrating to find out that your child "forgot" to give you the important message from Ms. What's-Her-Name.

Another telephone I have found to be essential to my business is a cellular phone. The benefits are many: My children can reach me at the same phone number every day, even though I have moved from job to job, and I can place or receive phone calls on a job site without using my client's phone. If I happen to get lost or am late to a business appointment, a simple telephone call can keep me out of hot water.

Organizing the Home Office

Controlling paperwork clutter is at the top of my list when it comes to staying organized. If you do not establish a good filing system right off the bat, you will be swimming in papers within no time: paint chips, addresses, client leads, magazine clippings, estimates, sketches and on and on. You will need a set of file folders to contain this paperwork blizzard, and a filing cabinet, drawer or box to contain the file folders.

Your filing system should contain folders for the following items.

1. *Each client.* Note name, address and directions to their house, as well as fax and telephone numbers, on the file folder. (I keep a notepad by the phone to write down this information during our initial phone conversation.) In this file you will keep specific instructions, paint colors, fabric swatches, sketches, samples, copies of proposal forms, billing statements and other pertinent data.

2. *Business documents.* These include your business plan, bank statements, tax returns, DBA forms and other business-related documents, as well as a file for insurance policies and forms so that you will always know where these documents are located.

3. *Business automobile records and mileage logs.*

4. *Receipts and expenses.* Make one folder for each year you are in business. If you have many receipts and expenses, I recommend an accordion file folder (but be sure the file is not too large to fit in your filing cabinet or file drawer) so you can subdivide the receipts into separate files labeled with the categories of your bookkeeping system, as discussed in chapter two. Also include a subfile for income, to hold check stubs and other records. (Hopefully this will be the fattest file yet!)

5. *Advertising.* Clip your own ads and any other advertisements that seem to jump off the page at you. These ads have impact and are worth clipping for future reference. Keep copies of all your ads, as well as a record of how well the ad performed. Also keep the various rate sheets, deadline agendas and advertising contracts required by various newspapers and magazines you advertise in.

6. *Ideas and inspiration.* Clip magazines articles, advertisements with interesting painted surfaces in the background, greeting cards that strike you as great ideas for a mural—anything that strikes your fancy.

7. *Work pending.* This is where I place those clients that are going to

get back to me or that maybe I can get to later, or clients who are simply "pending" for whatever reason—any client not active enough to warrant an individual file.

Keeping Your Time Calendar

I find it helpful to keep a master calendar next to the telephone. Of course, this is useless if it isn't revised often and kept up to date. On this calendar I write everything down: appointments, painting schedules, promised dates for sample deliveries, my daughter's orthodontist appointment, notes to call people—everything. If I don't write it down, I don't remember it—and nothing makes you look so unprofessional as forgetting.

I also keep a "Week at a Glance" calendar with me at all times. In this smaller calendar, I can record dates while meeting with clients, and then when I return home I transfer the date to the master calendar. I also keep a record of my billable time (i.e., painting at Jones'—4 hours) and my nonbillable time (i.e., sample for Smith—1 hour) on this calendar. Because this calendar is always with me, I also find it a convenient place to record my travel mileage (i.e., painting at Jones'—25 miles). If you are going to deduct your business travel in terms of mileage ($\times$ cents per mile), you must keep a record of all your business-related travel, even if it's just a trip to the paint store. Some people find it helpful to keep a separate mileage log in the car, but I prefer to use my daily calendar.

Record Keeping

Keep your business ledger in your office so that you always know where it is. Record keeping is the bane of my existence, but it is a very necessary evil. Do not let the task build up—update your records often so that the task does not loom larger than life. Even recording your bookkeeping data on a sheet of notebook paper is better than nothing. If you have a computer, I recommend using one of the many bookkeeping programs available. Choose one that is easy for you to use, but be sure to invest the time to learn the program properly, and enter the data into the computer often.

Creating the Studio/Work Space

Aside from the office space that you carved out for yourself, you must have a work area for painting. In a perfect world, this area would be a part of your office, but most of us are not nearly so lucky to have an area that is easily accessible and that can remain messy without endangering the family heirlooms. Personally, I believe that basements, garages and attics were meant to be places artists could claim as their own—and although these make excellent painting areas, they are gruesome office spaces. My solution was to use a spare room in my house as the office and to take over a good portion of my garage for my work space/studio. I had cabinets, peg boards and shelving units installed to store paints and supplies. Living in Chicago, it was also imperative that I have it heated, and I made sure the lighting was sufficient (so I wouldn't go blind within the first month). Because the setup is so efficient, I can store all my equipment out there and still have room for the usual garage paraphernalia, like my car.

You must have a place to make samples, to experiment with color, to work out a new stencil design or to practice your brushstrokes. If you have to store everything away, out of sight, it will never get used, but being disorganized will hamper any creative flow and make your painting time miserable. Store your paints, supplies and equipment neatly labeled and organized so that you can grab whatever it is you need without hunting. I have an inordinate fondness for my paintbrushes, so I like to have them out, within easy reach, on my worktable. I keep them in colorful mugs, sorted by style and type of brush.

To keep things handy and you sane, use tape or Velcro to attach a plastic cup to your ladder for holding brushes, pencils and small rulers. This can avoid wasting time and energy hunting for that pencil you set down somewhere.

A sturdy worktable and/or drafting table is a great addition to the studio. A comfortable stool or chair that fits your body to the work space helps relieve stress and strain on the muscles. A floor covering that provides cushioning and warmth can be an added bonus. Good lighting is important to reduce eyestrain. And you should have a source of music to soothe and inspire you while you create.

Decorative painters who specialize in painted furniture, floorcloths or other craft items require a larger work area, because often these projects are large and must be finished in the studio, not in someone's home. Ideally, your work area should be large enough to separate the messy prepwork painting from the fine-finishing work. Sometimes you even need an extra space to use as a showroom for your finished products and for meeting with clients seeking custom work. Create an environment that works for you.

I like to fill my work environment with color and life, because I spend long hours there. My shelves are filled with colorful plastic containers and organizers to keep my supplies handy and organized. The walls are covered in funky posters and clippings I find amusing. It is also a good idea to have a bulletin board to post reminders of the status of work in progress, inspirational advice and good cartoons in your studio/work space. And during my busy seasons, I post pictures of my children there so I can remember what they look like.

A Checklist of Office Supplies and Equipment

Office Environment

Desk or Worktable
Telephone & Answering Machine
Filing Cabinet & File Folders
Large Master Calendar
Small "Week-at-a-Glance"
Calendar
Ledger Book

Workspace Environment

Worktable

Colorful Bins & Containers

Good Lighting

Stool or Chair

Source of Music

Decorative Painting Supplies and Equipment

There are surprisingly few tools and materials truly necessary to get your business started. Note that I said *truly necessary*, because I have accumulated quite a collection of supplies and equipment over the years. Some of what I have accumulated I could not live without, but some of these items are totally useless. Because of my obsession with color, I love paints—I own practically every color of the little 2 oz. (62.2g) acrylic craft paint bottles (three large drawers full), hundreds of tubes of acrylic and oil paints, jars of precolored glazes and shelves loaded with quart cans of fun paint colors. I also own over 40 stencil brushes in various makes and sizes, three containers of fine-art brushes, a pegboard full of different types of wall painting brushes and lots of specialty brushes for faux finishing. I suspect I own hundreds of stencils and other materials. My collection of tools could rival *Tool-Time*'s Tim Allen, especially when it comes to ladders—at last count I have four A-frames, three articulating ladders and one extension ladder, plus all the ladder attachments, jacks and planks you can imagine. I'm a sucker for every gadget and widget that comes along: Some have been marvelous finds, making my life a little easier, and others have been out-and-out duds, making me wonder what possessed me to buy them. I even have some products in their original packaging, never opened or used, on the off chance that if the day ever comes, I'll have exactly what I need. Fortunately for you, this list can be chiseled down to a small percentage of the junk I have collected; if you, too, are compulsive about paint supplies, happy shopping!

Tools of the Trade

Ladders

You must have a good, sturdy, lightweight ladder that you feel comfortable climbing, because you will be spending long periods of time contorting on it, carrying it, moving it and hanging off it. A good ladder is the number one essential piece of equipment if you are going to be painting walls. Obviously, if you choose to market hand-painted floorcloths or custom-painted furniture, a ladder is not going to be your top priority. And you won't need as many ladders as I've accumulated trying to find the "perfect" one. But be sure that the ladder you choose is sturdy, the rungs are broad enough to make your feet comfortable, and there aren't any sharp edges that will dent your body when you lean against it.

There are platform-type ladders that are excellent for stenciling, and articulating ladders that are excellent for wall glazing. You may find you need planks, and jacks to attach those planks to your ladder, if you are going to be working on lots of two-story walls. Just be sure that the ladder fits your body and feels safe under your feet. An important tip: Put a rubber mat under the ladder to keep the ladder from slipping when working on wood floors or stairs.

Drop Cloths and Tarps

A good supply of canvas tarps (drop cloths) and rolled plastic are a must for protecting carpets and floors from paint. You can make do with Aunt Bertie's old curtains, but it doesn't give a very professional look to your work site. Watch for your local home center's or paint store's annual "stock-up sale," as that is when you'll get the best price on canvas drop cloths. I suggest having enough to cover the entire floor of the room. I own four 4′ × 12′ (1.2m × 3.7m) runners, two 8′ × 12′ (2.4m × 3.7m) cloths and one huge 14′ × 20′ (4.3m × 6.1m) tarp. Use the rolled plastic to cover any furniture left in the room.

Any time you have a paint container open, cover all surfaces. Even if it's only for a little touch-up or a dab of paint, cover all surfaces. It only takes one drip to ruin the floor covering or nearby furniture. I keep a tarp under all my supplies, because cans could be drippy or simply dirty.

Supply Containers/Carriers

Carryalls or bins for toting supplies to and from job sites are essential to keep things neatly organized and to help you avoid making fifty trips to your car. I have two large bifold-topped plastic bins: one for my stenciling and mural painting supplies, and another for my faux finishing tools and supplies (see the Master Supply Lists). In each bin I keep a small toolbox filled with miscellaneous tools and equipment. Another smaller, sturdier carrier is handy for paints and painting media. These items can all be purchased at those wonderful specialty container stores in bright, fun colors.

Brushes

I am a stickler for buying the best quality brushes available for the task at hand. Nothing is more frustrating than struggling to try and make a poor-quality brush produce top-quality work: It isn't possible. Do not skimp when budgeting for brushes. I suggest owning at least 20 to 30 stencil brushes in various sizes so you don't have to worry about washing and drying time. There are many wonderful brushes and tools necessary to accomplish a faux finish or create a glazed wall finish. You will achieve far superior results when you use the finest quality tools available. Strokework and hand painting will be easier and more successful if the brushes you use are appropriate for the medium you are using. Again, good-quality artist brushes will produce better results.

Now that's not to say there isn't a use for "cheap" brushes. I have a good supply of chip brushes (great for stippling corners when wall

To clean acrylic paint out of brushes, soak the brushes for at least an hour in rubbing alcohol, and then wash with Murphy Oil Soap and a plastic brush scrubber (a plastic disk with small spikes coming up from the disk).

glazing), scruffy old artist brushes (great for painting animal fur) and splayed old toothbrushes (great for spattering).

Painting on walls is hard on artist brushes, and their life expectancy won't be what it would be if you were painting on a more forgiving surface such as paper, fabric or canvas. Be sure to replace spent brushes as needed, but never throw away an old brush—simply find a new purpose for it.

Tape

Tape is another essential tool of the trade, whether used for holding up your stencil, for painting stripes or for protecting (masking out) surfaces that are to remain unpainted. While there are many different types of tape on the market, it is important to find the one that works best in your climate. Humidity and temperature affect how well a tape will stick (or not). Ideally, your tape should stick well enough to stay up on the wall, but not so well that it pulls up the base coat of paint. Taping off all areas that are not to be painted is essential: Nothing will spoil a painted finish more than sloppy edges or overspray.

I own a tape gun or masking machine. This handy gadget applies masking tape to a roll of nonadhesive brown paper [available in different widths, but I prefer the 6″ (15cm)]. As you pull it from the gun, the tape sticks to the edge of the brown paper, giving you a now-adhesive paper mask. I use this tape-gun tape to protect all the doors, windows and trim where paint could drip. I find it especially useful to tape using this combination of tape and paper, as it is an excellent way to protect the carpet next to the baseboards. The drop cloths often like to pull away from the wall as you walk on them, but because the paper overhangs the baseboard where it meets the carpet, the paper provides extra protection should the tarps shift.

Some tapes keep a crisp, straight edge; others seem to stretch or leak. Paper tape, with one edge that is already adhesive, will make a crisp line at the ceiling if there is no molding, but doesn't stick well to painted or varnished trim. Because this tape is only adhesive on one side of the paper, it isn't appropriate for stripes. White, easy-release painter's tape is best for taping stripes. If the tape is going to remain on the walls for more than a few hours, use blue, "long-mask" painter's tape.

The giant do-it-yourself home stores generally have the best prices on tape, unless you can find a stock-up sale.

Paints, Glazes and Media

Obviously, as a decorative painter, you will need a ready supply of paint. If you are a gifted colorist and can mix colors reliably, you will need only a few bottles of primary colors and some toning colors. However, whether stenciling, freehand painting or faux finishing, be sure to have enough of all paint colors necessary to complete the entire project.

A complete set of colorants (universal tints) for adjusting colors will come in handy. I keep a set of colorants in my work box just in case I have to adjust a color on the job site.

Glazes are added to the paint to make it more translucent and to extend the open (working) time of the paint. There are many types of glazing media available, since most major paint companies now make both latex and alkyd glazing liquids. Paint conditioners are a product that can be added to paint to make the paint flow easier. All-purpose sealers are useful in helping paint bond to surfaces that do not readily accept paint. Fabric medium can be added to acrylic craft paints to make the paint dry soft, remain supple when dry and hold up better to laundering. Varnishes, primers, extenders and pearly mediums are also handy to have on hand.

Palettes and Buckets

Disposable paper palettes are a supply I cannot live without. These come in pads, like paper, but are polycoated (waxed) on one side and paper on the other. These pads are convenient and easy to carry, and cleanup is a snap—simply throw the used sheet away. These palettes fit handily into the shelf of most A-frame ladders, which is convenient for stenciling. Plastic food trays, available at warehouse stores in bulk supply for a bargain price, also make handy palettes. I find it necessary to tape or Velcro these trays to my ladder so they don't fall off. Do not try to recycle Styrofoam meat trays, because these cannot ever be cleaned enough to be safe and bacteria free.

When mixing a wall glaze, I place a disposable plastic bucket liner inside a regular one-gallon bucket and then place both buckets in a larger five-gallon bucket. This larger bucket catches all the drips. Using bucket liners eliminates the need for cleaning buckets—I just throw them away when I'm finished, making cleanup a snap!

Another handy tool if I am going to be working from a scaffold is a paint hook that attaches my bucket to the ladder or plank. Having the paint bucket attached to the ladder eliminates a lot of trips down to reload. I keep another empty bucket with a liner handy to hold soggy glazing tools, which helps keep the work area clean and the tools contained and out of my walking path. This too can be attached to the ladder with a paint hook.

When I am freehand painting and need to keep my brushes wet, I use a handy gadget made by Plaid Enterprises called a Brush Basin. It is a square shallow bucket with holes along the edges for holding brushes and a ribbed bottom for gently rinsing paint out of the brush. This can be attached to the ladder with Velcro pads.

Personal Supplies

There are supplies that aid me personally one the job. Topping my list are Nitrile gloves, which I wear to protect my skin and hands (these heavier gloves don't melt or dissolve when using oil paints). Your skin is your body's largest organ, so always wear gloves to protect it, even if you think the paints are nontoxic. And please wear a mask—or better yet, a respirator—if you are using oil-based products or are spraying paints.

I always wear a full-size apron with pockets to protect my clothes. The pockets are handy to store stuff in, which helps keep me from wasting time hunting for my brush or pencil.

"Have the right tools for the right job; don't make your job any harder than it has to be."

—DEB METLER

I love to have music playing when I'm painting, and I have found a radio helps to keep the monotony at bay. Music affects mood: I find upbeat, rhythmic music helps me paint faster, and quiet, relaxing music helps mellow the mood when I am stressed. Wearing a set of headphones deters the client from being too chatty and can keep you from imposing your musical tastes upon others with whom you may be sharing the work site.

Snacks and beverages keep energy sustained high enough to finish the job in a timely manner. Try to drink lots of water while you are working: Fatigue is often caused by thirst as much as hunger.

Master Supply Lists

The master supply lists contain the items I suggest owning so you can have the necessary equipment handy to complete any given task. You can compile your own lists or add to mine. I find it helpful to own duplicates of some supplies, keeping some in my studio/work space and some in my painting containers, which I take to every job. This saves me lots of time packing and unpacking supplies, and spares me lots of aggravation. Anything that you use often—and find that it's never where you need it when you need it—is a supply you need to own duplicates of.

Summary

1. Set up an office space to separate your business life from your private life.
2. Install a separate business telephone line, with an answering machine so you can be sure to get your messages.
3. Control paperwork clutter by establishing a filing system.
4. Keep a master calendar, but carry a smaller calendar with you at all times.
5. Do your bookkeeping regularly and accurately.
6. Create a work space, a place to paint and to store your equipment.
7. Use the master supply lists to stock up on the supplies you need.

Master List of Supplies and Equipment

Wall Glazing and Faux Finishing

TOOLS IN TOOLBOX
  pencils and pens
  permanent marking pens
  artist gum eraser
  paint bucket ladder hooks
  sanding block
  small straight rulers and triangles
  30 ft (9.1m) measuring tape
  screwdrivers (flat and Phillips)
  pliers
  hammer
  putty knife
  palette knife
  wire brush for brush cleaning
  Q-tip swabs
  Scotch tape
  scissors
  craft knife and blades
  utility knife
  artist's flat brush
  foam brush
  chalk line
  plastic or wooden stirrers
  spackle
  spare batteries (radio and camera flash)

MIXING MATERIALS
  buckets (large and small)
  bucket liners
  wooden stir sticks
  disposable plates/trays
  measuring utensils

JOB EQUIPMENT
  stepladders
  articulating ladders
  planks and ladderjacks
  extension cords
  folding worktable
  canvas drop cloths and tarps
  rolled plastic tarps for furniture
  T-square
  plastic level ruler
  yardstick
  extra lighting and bulbs

TAPE
  tape dispenser (gun)
  rolled paper for dispenser
  1″ (25mm) masking tape for dispenser
  long-mask blue masking tape
  easy-release painter's tape

PAINTING SUPPLIES
  paint
  paint tray and liners
  roller and roller covers
  paintbrushes (old and new)
  chip brushes (for edges aznd corners)
  faux finishing tools and specialty brushes
  assorted artist's brushes
  brush basin/water container
  foam brushes
  glazing media/paint conditioners
  mineral spirits
  rubbing alcohol
  universal tints
  sponges (natural and cellulose)
  box of rags
  empty containers with lids
  fan deck of paint chip colors

CLEANUP
  paper towels
  hand towel
  plastic wrap
  plastic bags
  brush soap
  hand cleaner
  stain remover
  trash bags
  Murphy Oil Soap (for brushes)
  wire brush
  Pledge
  Dust Buster

PERSONAL SUPPLIES
  gloves
  apron
  kneepads
  food/water
  chocolate
  toilet paper and tissue
  hair bands/hat
  radio
  Band-Aids
  ibuprofen
  breath mints
  hand cream

BUSINESS
  business cards
  proof of insurance
  portfolio
  invoice forms
  client file
  samples
  camera, flash and film
  note paper

Master List of Supplies and Equipment

Stenciling and Freehand Painting

TOOLS IN TOOLBOX
  pencils and pens
  permanent marking pens
  artist gum eraser
  sanding block
  small straight rulers and triangles
  30 ft. (9.1m) measuring tape
  screwdrivers (flat and Phillips)
  pliers
  palette knife
  brush scrubber for brush cleaning
  Q-tip swabs
  Scotch tape for stencil repair
  Scissors
  craft knife and blades
  utility knife
  artist's brush for touchups
  foam brushes
  chalk line and chalk
  plastic or wooden stirrers
  spare batteries (radio and camera flash)

JOB EQUIPMENT
  opaque projector and stand
  stepladders
  planks and ladder jacks
  extension cords
  folding worktable
  canvas drop cloths and tarps
  rolled plastic tarps for furniture
  T-square
  plastic-bubble level ruler
  assorted rulers and yardstick
  extra lighting and bulbs

TAPE
  tape dispenser, paper and masking tape
  long-mask blue masking tape
  1″ (25mm) masking tape
  easy-release tape

PAINTING SUPPLIES
  Stencils, templates, patterns and sketches
  extra Mylar or stencil plastic
  tracing paper
  stencil cutting tools and glass or cutting board
  paint
  paint extender or mixing medium
  palette tray or pad
  clean disposable trays or plates
  assorted artist's brushes
  stencil brushes, assorted sizes
  brush basin/water container
  solvent (mineral spirits and rubbing alcohol)
  ppaper towels
  base coat paint for touchups
  paintbrushes (for bigger touchups—heaven forbid!)

CLEANUP
  hand towel
  rags
  plastic bags
  brush soap
  hand cleaner/soap
  Murphy Oil Soap (for brushes)
  plastic scrubber for stencil cleaning
  Dust Buster
  Pledge (for wood trim)
  trash bags

PERSONAL SUPPLIES
  gloves
  apron
  kneepads
  food/water
  chocolate
  Kleenex and/or toilet paper
  hair bands/hat
  radio
  Band-Aids
  ibuprofen
  breath mints
  hand cream

BUSINESS
  business cards
  proof of insurance
  portfolio
  stencil catalogs
  invoice forms
  client file
  samples and sketches
  camera, flash and film
  note paper

Chapter 4

Marketing Your Business

The next hurdle to cross is marketing yourself and your business. Some people naturally understand the art of marketing (born salesman that they are), but for others it is the most difficult part of the business. Many decorative painters I know are very shy, overly humble about their talents, and find it very difficult to market themselves and their business. Most people wrongly assume that marketing skills are driven by ego, but being egotistical and knowing how to market yourself are two very different concepts. You are marketing a product, your skill, talent and knowledge, so obviously the ego will have some stake in the process. I was often uncomfortable with the idea of promoting myself. I overcame this by playing a little mind game with myself that allowed my ego to step aside and let me practice the art of marketing, telling myself I am marketing the business rather than myself.

You simply *must* get your work and your business name known and out there. No business can survive, much less prosper, without marketing tactics, and a decorative painting business is no exception.

I like to think of marketing in terms of gardening—prepare the soil, plant the seeds, nurture the young plant, feed and cultivate it often and watch it grow. While not all seeds will flourish, with care, most seedlings will produce a bountiful harvest!

Stenciling, Etc.

Carole Haines Shearer, CS

18901 Orchard Terrace Road, Hagerstown, Maryland 21742 • (301) 733-0723

Sample letterhead

North Shore Wall Design
Decorative Painting

MURALS • STENCILING • FAUX FINISHES

Lynette Harris
(847) 853-0904

1023 OAKWOOD AVENUE
WILMETTE, IL 60091

PEGGY EISENBERG

Stencils With Style
Custom Decorative Stenciling

Lynette Slivinski

3379 Bear Creek Drive
Newbury Park, CA 91320   (805) 498-9890

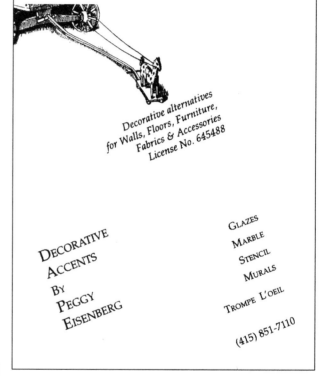

Decorative alternatives for Walls, Floors, Furniture, Fabrics & Accessories
License No. 645488

DECORATIVE ACCENTS BY PEGGY EISENBERG

GLAZES
MARBLE
STENCIL
MURALS
TROMPE L'OEIL

(415) 851-7110

ILLUSIONS OF GRANDEUR
DECORATIVE PAINTING
Stencilling. Wall Painting
Faux Finishes. Trompe l'oeil

Lynette Slivinski   Mary Jane Fisher
(805) 498-9890   (805) 492-1422

Stenciling, Etc.

Custom Stenciling
Walls • Wood • Fabric
Decorative Wall Finishes

Carole Haines Shearer, CS
(301) 733-0723

Betty's Art Barn

Betty Chapman
Artist

679 S. 10000 W Rd.
Bonfield, IL 60913
(815) 426-6337

Business cards

44

Marketing Tactics

Developing a marketing strategy can seem overwhelming, but it can be accomplished by following a few simple steps.

Business Cards

Business cards are an important marketing tool. Your business cards should reflect your personality and the style of your business. The card can be simple: your name, your company name, address, telephone number and a brief description of the services you offer. Or the card can be elaborate, colorful, hand-cut to an unusual shape or oversized into a folding shape, with original artwork or photography. These more elaborate cards can be costly but very effective: Just be sure you don't get so wrapped up in the artistic aspect of your business cards that you forget the essential data: name, address, telephone number and services offered.

Keep a stack of business cards with you at all times. Having extra cards in the glove compartment of your car will help ensure that you have some available, even if the supply in your purse or wallet is used up. Keep business cards in your work boxes for people who visit the work site. Enclose a business card with every correspondence, and leave extra business cards (for referrals) with each client after completing the job.

A Portfolio of Your Work

Your most visual marketing tool will be your professional-quality portfolio. Your portfolio should make the viewer sit up and say, "Wow!" Your portfolio should contain your resume (a written definition of your credentials), proof of insurance and business licenses, colorful and well-painted samples, high-quality photographs, press clippings featuring your work, and any accolades, awards, accreditation or certification documentation. Your portfolio serves to give your client confidence that you do indeed have

North Shore Wall Design

D E C O R A T I V E   P A I N T I N G

Lynette Harris • 123 First Street • Wilmette, Illinois 60000
Phone (847) 555-5555 • Fax (847) 555-5555 • e-mail: MLHarris57@aol.com

North Shore Wall Design specializes in paint finishes for walls, floors, ceilings and furniture. Award-winning artist, Lynette Harris, owner of *North Shore Wall Design*, creates master-quality decorative painting for home or office. Lynette's work has been featured in numerous Designer Showcase homes and published in *Better Homes & Garden's Windows and Walls, House Beautiful Kitchens & Baths, North Shore Magazine, Decorating Retailer, The Artistic Stenciler* and the *Chicago Home Book*. Lynette Harris is the author of *Making Money With Your Creative Paint Finishes,* by North Light Books.

FAUX FINISHES:

Wall Glazes:	Parchment Finish, Positive & Negative Finishes and Colour Wash
Marble:	Travertine, Verde, Tinos, Drift Marble and Fantasy Faxu
Stone:	Granite, Fossilstone, Stone Block and Brick

DECORATIVE PAINTING:

Murals:	Trompe L'oeil, Children's Rooms and Architectural
Stenciling:	Master-Quality Free-Form Designs, Borders and Graphics
Floors:	Painted Wood, Cement Porches, Stairs and Faux Rugs
Ceilings:	Skyscapes, Architectural Medallions & Crown Moldings
Furniture:	Finish Details, Ornamentation & Decoration

Sample resume

the skill, experience and knowledge to complete the commission.

When I present my portfolio, I like to think I am inviting the client to walk through a garden alive with color and texture, a visual feast that is pleasing, inspiring and captivating.

Do not be deterred if you do not have a lot of experience and accreditation. There are many ways a beginner can assemble an effective portfolio. Even with only a few completed projects under your belt, you can create a dazzling portfolio.

1. Start with a smaller portfolio, because smaller pages are easier to fill.
2. Type up a list of services offered, or a resume if skills and training warrant one.
3. Place all business-related documentation (proof of insurance, painting organization affiliations, accreditations or educational certificates) at the beginning. This is a good place to include a self-portrait of you at work to lighten the seriousness of the business documents.
4. Take clear, well-focused photographs of each completed project and make enlargements. Also use photos showing close-up details.
5. Use before-and-after pictures to illustrate the dramatic difference decorative painting makes to a room setting. Show a painted sample of the finish used.
6. Make subtle glazed background pages to form a spectacular backdrop for your photographs.
7. Include any sketches used for a mural or trompe l'oeil, along with a photo of the completed project.

Even established decorative painters tend to make mistakes with their

Don't be afraid to use the walls of your house as photo opportunities. Take "before" pictures, paint your project and photograph the completed work "after" to show how decorative painting can enliven a blank wall. Even if this work isn't something you wish to live with, you can paint out the wall and have a fresh palette for another project.

portfolios. Here are some of the pitfalls you will want to avoid.

1. Small, dark or poor-quality photographs that do not do the work justice. All photographs should be in focus, well lighted and at least 5″×7″ (13cm×18cm) but 8″×10″ (20cm×25cm) is preferable.

2. Too many or too few photographs. You don't want to overwhelm potential clients by showing them everything you've ever painted, nor do you want to underwhelm your audience by showing fewer than a dozen photos.

3. Poorly painted samples or dirty, battered pages. Remember, this book represents the quality of your work.

4. Old, outdated work. Your portfolio should be updated frequently.

I know several decorative painters who carry a mini-portfolio with them at all times. This little book fits into their purse or pocket and can be whipped out at a moment's notice. It is very effective for explaining ''Just What It Is That You Do.'' A quick-look book is a great way to keep smaller photographs of your current work handy while you wait for the enlargements necessary to update your portfolio. It is also a highly effective networking tool.

A Networking Strategy

The single most effective tool for marketing your business is to network, network, network. The dictionary defines *networking* as the informal sharing of information or services. I define networking as knowing when to toot your own horn. The following are some ideas of the many ways to network.

1. Write a press release announcing the opening of your new business

---

I have two portfolios: one for stenciling and murals, and the other for wall glazing and faux finishing. Both of these have been whittled down to the bare bones, the best of the best, because otherwise it takes too long to show the portfolio to the client.

and send it to every local publication. Be sure to include a photo to entice the editors. (See sample press release on page 56.)

2. Deliver or mass-mail printed fliers. Again, photos sell, so consider using a color copy in your flier. New housing construction or subdivisions can be an excellent area to target.

3. Have a spectacular photo made into a postcard and send it to all the interior designers in your area. This postcard can announce your presence, or simply remind the designers that you're available to create something wonderful for them, too.

Any mailings to professional contacts, such as interior designers or builders, should end with an invitation for a consultation and portfolio viewing. All letters should be followed up with a telephone call within a week.

4. Prepare a mini-portfolio of painted samples and copies of photographs to leave with local design studios, contractors, builders or shopkeepers who you trust to promote your talents. Make sure your business name and phone number are prominently featured and on every photo and sample board.

5. Host a coffee for designers, architects, builders, contractors and shop owners for a presentation of your work. A short slide presentation works well.

6. Paint a showcase home, model home or other public setting (library, storefront, restaurant or doctor's office) for free. Painting where many people can see your work is a terrific way to get your work seen by many people. Another great place to get noticed is to paint (gratis) anywhere women spent a lot of time: hair or nail salons, decorating centers, workout spas, tailor shops, day-care centers or school facilities, baby stores, furniture or antique stores and pediatricians' offices. Sign your work and be sure to arrange to have your cards on display, or get permission to hang a framed card or resume so it's permanently attached to your artwork. If no one knows who did the painting, it isn't a very effective networking tool.

7. Get a magnetic sign for your vehicle. Turn your car into a rolling

advertisement. Hand-painting one of these signs makes for an extra attention grabber. Having a personalized license plate is another fun networking idea, and your license plate frame can be painted to accentuate it.

8. Join the Chamber of Commerce and any other local business organizations you have time for: These organizations are for networking. Call your local government offices to find out if your city, or a city nearby, has a Chamber of Commerce.

9. Donate your time and talents to the local elementary schools. Children love to paint. Be sure to attach a business card to each child's project.

10. Get a booth at local art festivals or community fairs. Have a colorful flier to hand out, as well as lots of painted samples and photos on display.

11. Join decorative painting groups. Networking with other decorative painters can recharge those creative batteries and open new doors. (See Appendix, page 146.)

The most important point about networking is to talk about what you do as often as possible to anyone and everyone. Don't be shy. And get out there and paint. Like a snowball rolling downhill, the more painting you do, the more exposure you will have, because more people will see your work. So, paint your own house, your friends' houses, your family's houses, your spouse's office and the dog's house.

Advertising Strategies

Advertising your business is an important aspect of promoting yourself and inducing the public to call. While I feel strongly that the best advertising is word of mouth from a happy client, there comes a time when you must make a public announcement regarding your business.

Work for free when given a chance to paint in a public place where your work will get a lot of attention. Having a commercial site to showcase your best work will do more for your business than a year's advertising.

Print Advertising

There are many public mediums for advertising, but since decorative painting is a visual art, printed advertisements in the local newspapers, regional magazines, mass-mailers and printed fliers will be the most effective. While the obvious point of running a printed ad is to get the phone to ring with job offers, the long-term goal of advertising should be name recognition. Again, think of advertising as planting the seed. Sometimes it takes a long time to harvest the results.

I have received phone calls from people who clipped my ad and kept it for months before they were ready to call. Try not to be disappointed if you don't get a lot of phone calls after spending a lot of money on a classified ad.

Advertising is expensive, but budgeting advertising costs into a newly established business is important to develop recognition, establish your credibility and reach the largest public audience possible. Since advertising is costly, your printed ad must be as effective as possible. You won't know how effective your ad is until you've placed it several times, so some trial and error is inevitable.

A printed ad must grab the reader's attention. Your ad will need to leap off the page and demand attention. The tendency is to put the company name (or your name) in the boldest print, but this is a mistake. Let the artwork catch the eye first. The visual impact of the advertisement must make the reader stop and take a closer look. Use artwork and pictures—an exciting advertisement can be rarely be accomplished with written copy alone.

The size of the ad is important, too. A larger advertisement will carry more punch than a small ad that is lost among the print, so budget for a larger ad rather than running several small ones. The most effective advertisement I ever placed was a black-and-white photograph of a stenciled mural with a bare minimum of written copy underneath.

Your ad should run as often as your budget will allow throughout the first few years of establishing your business. There are times when one ad will be more effective than others (poor placement, a warm sunny day after a week-long rainstorm, tax or vacation season and so on). If, after running the ad two or three times, you have received few or no phone calls, it's time to redesign the ad or consider another publication. The timing and placement of your ad within the pages of the paper or magazine can make a big difference in its success. Decorating tends to be cyclical—in my area it's most popular during the spring and before the winter holidays, so ads placed just prior to those months will be more productive than ads placed during the summer. Check with your local newspaper about special decorating editions or home improvement supplements: These are the best vehicles in which to advertise your business.

The written copy of the advertisement must be clear and easy to read. Decisively state what you are selling, so that the reader does not have to struggle to understand your ad. Use "power" words, such as *free*, *new* and *limited-time offer*. Use fonts that are different from the publication's usual typeface. Remember that building name recognition is your primary goal, so always be sure your business name is eye-catching.

Every advertisement should reflect your style and business objectives. If your goal is to reach an upscale clientele, your ad must be refined and elegant. If you are eager to specialize in children's rooms, your ad should playfully reflect a sense of whimsy.

Suggested advertising mediums include

• Newspapers
• Mass-mailed advertising supplements
• Coupon booklets
• Local or regional magazines
• Yellow pages in area telephone books
• Church bulletins
• School bulletins

Fliers and brochures

Fliers and brochures are another fine way to promote the business. A flier is more informal than a brochure, and also more cost effective. Fliers should be colorful and inviting. Again, the artwork and photographs will speak for themselves, but because you will have more space available, the wording must be creative to entice the reader. To hold the reader's attention, work under the premise that "less is more."

But take care, when distributing fliers, to target the correct marketplace, rather than just willy-nilly putting them everywhere. When I first started my stenciling business, I put together a one-page flier and hired children to deliver them around my neighborhood. Looking back, I know this wasn't the best way to target clients, because these people were not necessarily looking for my services. Needless to say, I didn't get a single phone call. I would have made better use of the effort and expense by targeting a new housing development.

A printed brochure can be as elaborate as your budget will allow. Some decorative painters have a simple, yet elegant, three-fold single page; others have a printed folder binding several pages of artwork, photographs, resumes and credentials. Each, in its own way, is a very effective promotional tool.

My style was to split the difference between a formal brochure and a colorful flier. I took a dozen photographs of what I considered my best work and mounted them on plain white paper with computer-typed explanations underneath. I ran these photograph pages through a color copier, used my resume for the cover and then had them bound. Because the photographs speak for themselves, it has been very well received.

Promotional Letters and Direct Mailings

A well-written letter of introduction directed to a target audience is another very productive marketing technique. An impressive, enticing letter full of enthusiasm, coupled with a photograph or two, can work better than any printed advertisement. In this letter you will want to present yourself in an "Oh wow, I'm here and are you lucky to find me!" style.

The overall length of the letter should not exceed one page. Your first paragraph must grab readers: Hit them with a catchy opening line. The bulk of the letter should be clear, concise and to the point. Although you should never lie, with a little thought, your credentials can be presented in a most creative manner.

Catchphrases you might use include

- "A high level of expertise and attention to detail"
- "I use only the finest materials."
- "Faux finishes give depth and character to any wall surface and make an excellent background for painted ornamentation."
- "Master-quality . . ."
- "My stenciling style has outgrown the rigid mindset of repeated ducks and pineapples. Today's stencils are more free-form and artistic, using trompe l'oeil techniques and freehand embellishments to achieve a more painterly look."

High-quality photographs can be made into postcards and mailed to a target audience. This visual feast will entice the reader. These postcards can also be handed out at networking events. Again, the postcards are a visual message and, as such, are a very effective marketing tool.

Suggested target market for letters of introduction include

- Interior designers
- Home decorating centers
- Contractors, builders and developers
- Architects
- Painting contractors
- Paint and wallpaper stores
- Furniture stores
- Unfinished furniture stores
- Baby furniture stores
- Antique stores
- Specialty and gift shops
- Restaurants

Keep track of how your clients find you so that you know which marketing strategies work best for you.

Always follow up any direct mailing with a telephone call. The feedback you get is invaluable in determining the success of your advertisement.

Signage

Signs used to display your business name can be very effective, because they are another visual form of advertising. A free-swinging metal sign can be placed at each job site. Be sure to ask permission from the client before using their property for your advertising.

Using your work vehicle to display advertising is another way build name recognition. Lots of people tell me, "I've seen your car about town." Magnetic signs can be painted in an eye-catching manner, and you can have a personalized (vanity) license plate to promote your business.

Free Publicity

Most newspapers are interested in articles on decorative painting, as such articles make for interesting reading. Contact the editor of the section your article would most likely fit into, such as the home or decorating sections. Offer to show editors your portfolio. I have found editors to be very busy people, and have had better luck with a letter of introduction, coupled with a few dazzling photographs, followed up by a telephone call. Some editors have been abrupt to the point of rudeness, but then have run the article anyway. Develop a thick skin and persevere.

A press release is another effective way to get free publicity. The local paper is your best bet for running a press release about you and your business. Announcing a new business in the community is always newsworthy!

While this announcement won't make most people run to the phone, it plants another seed to promote the business. Be creative: Lots of announcements are worthy of a press release.

Again, the best advertising is word of mouth from a satisfied customer, but that customer has to find you in the first place. Networking takes time. If you want a quick jump-start for your business, budget heavily for advertising and perform a media blitz.

WALL STENCILING BUSINESS OPENS

Lynette Slivinski, a former Southern California resident, has opened a new business in Wilmette, North Shore Wall Designs, which specializes in decorative painting for walls—subtle background glazes, master-quality stenciling, murals and total-room concepts. As a member of the Stencil Artisan's League, Slivinski has earned her master-level certification in wall stenciling. In addition, she has taught classes at national conventions, and several of her original designs have been published.

Summary

1. You *must* get your work and your business name out there.
2. Have business cards printed showing your name, address, telephone number and a description of services offered by your business.
3. Prepare a showstopping portfolio, and carry a small quick-look book with you at all times.
4. Plan a networking strategy to toot your own horn, including writing press releases, delivering fliers, sending postcard photographs to interior designers, hosting a coffee to present a slide presentation of your work, painting a showcase house or public setting for free, turning your vehicle into a rolling advertisement and joining networking organizations.
5. Plan an advertising media blitz using printed advertising, fliers, brochures and promotional letters, and display eye-catching signage.
6. Take advantage of free publicity whenever possible.

Chapter 5

Pricing and Estimates

Pricing Your Work

Pricing work is by far the most controversial and subjective discussion among decorative painters. Pricing is an intensely personal subject. What may seem like an exorbitant billing rate to one decorative painter may be close to minimum wage to another. As much as I'd like to provide you with a magic formula for determining your pricing structure, it simply cannot be. Only you can nail down what your time and your product is worth. Therefore, you will have to do some introspective soul searching and some detective work. As a good starting point, take the time to answer the following questions.

1. How many hours am I going to work per day? Per week? How many of those hours will be billable?
2. How busy do I want—or need—to be?
3. Does my skill level demand top dollar, or should I charge less while I gain experience?
4. What is my minimum hourly wage? What is the absolute minimum I am willing to charge for loading the ladder and gathering my supplies?
5. What is the most amount of money I can hope to earn in one year?

What is the least I can afford to earn yearly?

6. What will the area I choose to work in allow me to charge? What will the market bear? Do I live in a high per capita income (urban) area, or is my working area more rural?

Time is money. . . . This old adage never feels truer than when you're hanging off the ladder with paint running down your arms. No matter whether you want to price your work by the hour, by the painting day, by the job or by the piece, the price you charge is determined by the amount of money earned in proportion to the amount of time spent. While you may not always be able to control the amount of time a particular project will take, or even to guess how long a job will take, you can take some of the guesswork out by working your pricing structure out well in advance of bidding for a job.

I had been in business for about ten years before I figured out my actual hourly billing rate. My billing practices were not haphazard, but I never stopped painting long enough to figure out how many hours I was working compared to how much I was billing. My prices were determined by the job: If I was stenciling, I figured my price by the linear foot (i.e., so much per foot of stenciling, determined by the number of stencil overlays and the number of colors used in the application), and if I was wall glazing, I determined my price by the square foot (i.e., so much per square foot of wall space determined by the type of process). As my painting style evolved—for example, when pricing a mural—this pricing system simply did not work. This forced me to sit down and examine the amount of time it truly took to paint a particular application, and what my true price per hour was. This number is simply a tool to help you estimate prices and gauge your pricing accuracy. I already had a figure bouncing around in my head of what my hourly rate might be, and was happily surprised when the results of this exercise came very close to that number.

If you are just starting out and do not have a schedule of work booked, you are probably saying to yourself, "But wait! I haven't even gotten a single job yet! I have no clue how much I'll be working or how long it's going to take me to paint *x, y* and *z.*'' Don't worry: For this exercise we are going to pretend that you have as much work booked as you can handle, because if you work hard at building your business, you will be as busy as you want, or need, to be.

When you are determining your hourly rate, it is also helpful to note all the time you spend before and after you actually work on the job, which includes buying and mixing paint, answering telephone calls, preparing sample boards, doing paperwork (preparing the estimate and sending your contract), consulting, purchasing supplies, gathering, loading and unloading your equipment, travel or driving time and cleanup time. While this time probably isn't included in your actual billing, it is all time you have invested to accomplish the job in question.

I had a client complain to me, ''You were only here painting for three hours. How can you charge so much?'' She did not understand the amount of work I had already put into her particular commission so that I could go into her home and paint quickly. When I gently explained to her all the work I had done besides the physical act of painting, she apologized, and we both felt better about the bill.

Timekeeping

I recommend that you keep a written log of all the time you spend working for several weeks. This log will include, for example, time you spend on the telephone, shopping for supplies, cleaning brushes or stencils, preparing boards, completing samples and paperwork (preparing the estimate, filing your notes and billing for the completed job), as well as actual painting time for each and every job. Be sure to be specific on your time entries, breaking the process into the smallest units possible. Most artists I know have trouble calculating their time, thus frustrating everyone involved. Because it's easy to get lost in a timeless world while merrily painting away, this exercise forces you to pay attention to the reality of time spent on a project, not wildly guess how long you *think* you've been working on it. After you have kept records of your time for a few weeks, you will have an invaluable tool for estimating your time for future jobs. For example, if it took you seven hours to glaze 400 square feet of wall space, plus four hours of nonbillable time (meeting the client, making samples, buying supplies, loading and unloading equipment and cleaning up), you now have a good basis for further estimates. Keeping track of your time is very important in determining your pricing structure.

Recording the time you spend on making samples is one way to get proficient at price estimating. If it takes you twenty minutes to stencil one repeat on the sample board, you have some idea of how complicated and time-consuming that pattern will be on the job site. Multiply that by the number of repeats required to complete the job, and you'll have a good idea of how long it will take you to stencil the room. If it takes you ten minutes to sponge the glaze onto a two-foot-square board, you can assume you can sponge one square foot in five minutes. You can then multiply that by the number of square feet of wall space. After multiplying the time by the number of repeats, I double the time estimate to include time spent setting up, mixing paint, taping off the room, climbing up and down the ladder and cleaning up. While this time estimate is still only a best guess, you now have information that can help you come closer to calculating your billable time.

Figuring Your Billing Rate

Bear with me here—I tend to break out in a clammy sweat and my mind shuts down when I have to do anything remotely resembling a ''story problem''—but if you are to have any hope of developing a pricing structure, you must do the math. Simple arithmetic is the only way to determine your hourly painting rate. It's essentially a seven-step process.

1. Determine the number of hours that will constitute your painting day.

Not everyone can work (paint) the same amount of hours during a workday. I can only paint a maximum of six or seven hours a day before I begin to tire and lose that creative spark, or before I get sloppy and make mistakes. Some days I reach my limit after four or five hours. I have learned it's important to know when to stop for the day, and have often regretted pushing myself when I was too tired to be effective. Of course, I have painted marathon hours to meet deadlines or when my calendar is overbooked, but this is the exception rather than the rule. Not physically painting a full eight- or nine-hour workday allows me time to return phone calls, buy supplies, meet with clients or do in-office work and still be able to have an intelligent conversation with my family that evening.

2. Determine the number of days that will constitute your workweek.

I know many decorative painters who only paint four days a week, leaving the fifth day open to see clients, make samples and do office work. Decide for yourself how many hours you are able to physically paint per week (your actual billable hours), being sure to include enough time to also build and maintain the business (your nonbillable hours).

3. Determine the number of weeks per year that will constitute your actual working time.

Now that you have figured out hour many hours a day constitute your painting day, ask yourself: How many weeks per year am I going to work? Subtract vacations and personal time off from the total weeks per year (52). Subtract at least two weeks per year for illness or emergencies. You will also need to subtract a few weeks for the inevitable times when business is slow, which I call downtime. It seems that there is a natural cycle to the work year, making some seasons busier than others. For me, my schedule is busiest from the day school starts until the holidays, and again in the spring before summer weather sets in and sends most of my clients outdoors. There will often be times when I will work extra days (during a real time crunch, I have worked seven days a week) or fewer days in any given week (when my calendar has been messed up or it's the dog days of summer), but having a norm to shoot for is extremely helpful in determining a pricing structure. So subtract a few weeks for downtime.

	52 weeks per year (FIVE DAY WORKWEEK)
minus	4 weeks for vacation and personal time off (MORE IF YOU PLAY GOLF)
minus	2 weeks for sick days (YOU MAY NEED MORE IF YOU HAVE SMALL CHILDREN)
minus	7 weeks for maintaining the business (ONE DAY PER WEEK)
minus	3 weeks for downtime
Leaving a total of	36 weeks per year of actual working time.

This figure may seem low, but there is the danger of burnout if you work much more than this in any given year.

4. Determine your expected annual income.

The next step will be to determine how much income you want and/or need to earn per year. Determine the highest annual income you can earn, and also determine the least annual income you can earn and still remain in business (no one wants to see red ink at the end of the year!).

5. Use mathematical equations to determine your billing rates.

First, figure your highest possible yearly income (hopeful, yet within reason). Take that figure and divide it by the number of weeks you plan on working (as determined in step 3 above), divide it again by the number of billable days per week (as determined in step 2 above) and then divide it again by the number of hours per day (as determined in step 1 above). This figure gives you the high-end hourly rate.

An example based on a $50,000 per year income:

$50,000 divided by 36 weeks	=	$1,388.00 per week
$1,388 divided by 4 days	=	$347.00 per day
$347 divided by 6 hours	=	$58.00 per hour

Second, figure your absolute minimum annual salary (the least you, your business and your family can survive on). Take that figure and divide it by the number of weeks you plan on working. Divide your weekly salary again by the number of billable hours per week. This gives you your minimum wage.

An example based on a $50,000 per year income:

$20,000 divided by 36 weeks	=	$556.00 per week
$555 divided by 4 days	=	$139.00 per day
$139 divided by 6 hours	=	$23.00 per hour

This is your lowball price for jobs you really want (you know, the ones you would probably be willing to pay to paint!), or a fair price while you are gaining experience.

6. Take into account regional pricing.

Another factor to consider when determining your pricing structure is the area of the country in which your business will be operating. The perceived value of your product will vary greatly from a metropolitan area to a rural community, and from the coasts to the heartland. To figure out what your community can afford and will be willing to pay for your services, you'll have to do a little detective work. Find out what other service industries charge for labor in your neighborhood. What do housepainters charge? Wallpaper hangers? Plumbers? And even better, what do other decorative painters in your area charge? You will have to be creative, as well as tactful, when asking for information regarding pricing. All of this data can be used to ascertain what clients in your area should be willing to pay for your services. Under no circumstances should your price be lower than housepainters or the wallpaper hangers, but I personally have yet to equal plumbers: Pick a price in between these two service-based businesses and check to see that it works with your business plan.

If you work in an area where your clientele is wealthy, you may have to charge even more for your work. These clients do not necessarily want the best deal—sometimes they want the best work and, in their minds, that equals the most expensive.

When we moved to Chicago, I continued to price my work the same as I had in Southern California and yet I kept losing jobs that I bid on. The area of Chicago I chose to work in was one of the more affluent areas in the country. It seems that I wasn't charging enough to interest the upper-crust clientele. These clients were more discriminating and wanted more exclusive work. I raised my prices, changed my attitude and began to book more jobs.

Of course, if you are in an area where there is a lot of competition, you will have to price your work competitively or you will lose jobs to your competitors.

7. How Busy Do You Want to Be?

The less you charge, the busier you will be. If you are after experience, there is absolutely nothing wrong with undercharging for your work. But keep in mind that people value what they pay for.

When I first started out, I was just happy to book the job—the pay was secondary. But after months of hearing, "You are so cheap!" and "You want a deal? Hire Lynette," it quickly grew old. I knew I needed to raise my prices. The final straw was when I overheard a decorator tell a client "not to hire [another decorative painter] because he was too exclusive; hire Lynette because she's so very reasonable." Hey, I wanted to be exclusive, too!

The reality was that as my confidence and experience grew, I began to value my time and sense of worth. I learned to adjust my price accordingly. However, every time I raised my prices some business fell away, and I worried that I had overpriced myself. Sure, I lost the clients who were only

"I try to give my client a little more than they expect so they will look back at our painting experience fondly."

—SHERI HOEGER

interested in a cheap decorating fix, but the clients I retained valued my services more. And it wasn't long before my calendar was just as full as it was before I raised my prices.

On the other hand, pricing yourself out of the market is a real concern. If you are constantly being underbid and losing jobs, you need to reevaluate the market to determine if it will bear your prices. Something that is overpriced is not marketable.

Preparing the Estimate

Now that you have figured out your billing and pricing structure, the next logical step is to determine how long it will take you to paint the job in question. Estimating the time factor of a job is by far the hardest part of decorative painting. Long-time professionals still struggle with this issue. Past experience to draw on helps make it easier, but every job has unknown factors that will affect the completion time. I often feel that an estimate should really be called a "guesstimate." Everyone paints at different speeds: What may take one person ten minutes to stencil might take another twenty, and still another only five minutes. There is no standard formula for estimating how long it will take to paint a particular application. Most customers seem more comfortable knowing exactly what the bottom-line costs will be, with few or no surprises at billing time.

Estimating a Job Price

There are several methods used to estimate a job price, such as quoting by the job, by measurement figures or by time and materials, but all methods end up using the same premise: How long it will take you to paint the particular area, plus the added cost of the materials. How you choose to

If you are getting every job you bid on, odds are good that your prices are too low.

determine the job price will be up to you: Use the method you feel most comfortable with.

Remember: Although the price of all work is based on the amount of time necessary to complete the job, the client should never be privy to your hourly rate, which is merely a necessary tool used in the process of bidding a job.

Quoting By the Job

This is the method I prefer for quoting a job price, because the end result, a specific painted finish, is the same for each job. There will be little or no haggling over how long it took to you to paint. This is very much a bottom-line method of pricing, which is always my preferred modus operandi. Of course, the risk involved here is that you miscalculated the time it takes to complete the job. I suppose I like living on the edge, because this is how I bid most of my jobs now.

To determine a by-the-job price, you will have to prepare samples of all finishes to be painted to determine a guesstimate of the billable time involved, being sure to add the expected non billable hours. If the job has some circumstances that will make it more difficult and time-consuming to complete, such as high ceilings or lots of doors and windows to tape off, multiply your expected number of hours by your highest billing rate. If the job is fairly straightforward, or perhaps you simply want the job because it will provide good exposure for your business, multiply the projected number of hours by your lower hourly rate. This will give you high-end and low-end dollar amounts for quoting a job price. After reviewing these numbers, you can make the call on what a fair-market value should be for this particular job. Next add the expected cost of materials and any referral fees, if needed. This total dollar amount is then quoted to the client on your proposal form (i.e., painted scene in master bathroom = $800).

Quoting By Measurement

This method requires an accurate linear or square footage measurement for all surfaces to be painted, and establishing your price-per-foot charge.

The room measurement is multiplied by your price per foot (i.e., stencil border of 40 linear feet×$10/ft. *or* 400 sq. ft. wall glazing×$2/ft.). Be sure to add the cost of materials. Quoting a price per foot is much like the per-job method, because you are basing your price per foot on how long it takes to paint that amount of linear or square footage. You could break down the fee on your proposal as such, 40 linear feet @ $10/ft., giving the client the opportunity to add or subtract footage from their quote depending on the budget. But I have found this to be a drawback when the client is only interested in shaving the cost of the job and ignoring what's best for the room setting. However, knowing how you reached your bid gives you and your client an opportunity to work together to stay within budget. Don't forget to add a materials charge and any other extra fees to the total per-foot charge.

Quoting By Time and Materials

The time and materials method is by far the most open-ended billing method. I have found very few clients who would be willing to allow me to work for them using this billing method. Simply stated, you tell the client, "I charge $X per hour (or I charge $X per painting day) and will bill materials at my cost." Naturally, the first question the client will ask is, "How long is this going to take?" And if you knew the answer to that question, you would be able to give a better estimate. That's the drawback of quoting a job based on time and materials. Some clients are willing to work within that parameter—but not many. However, there are times when this is the only way to bid a job, such as a job with so many variables that other bidding methods cannot be used. For example, it could be used for a job of such magnitude that you truly have no previous data from which to draw your estimate. I suggest that you arrange billing at regular intervals (like by the week) to avoid giving the client sticker shock.

Since I do not believe in telling the client my hourly billing rate, I find that if I am going to bid a job by this method, I prefer to give the client a price range (I can complete this job within the price range of $800 to $1,200 plus $30 to $60 for materials). Phrased this way, most clients are more willing to accept a time and materials quote. And as I got more experienced at determining how long various applications took to paint, I was able to offer the client a fairly close ballpark estimate that was more reassuring to the client and to me.

Additional Charges

Some jobs may require a percentage tacked onto the job price for what I call the "Pain-in-the-Rear Factor." I add 10 to 20 percent of the estimated job price to any job I suspect is going to give me a pain: an unpleasant client or designer, a detail-oriented client, high travel times or parking difficulties, tight construction/contractor schedules or deadlines, annoying pets, precocious small children or uncomfortable working conditions (no air conditioning, no working plumbing or poor lighting).

Always charge more for working on ceilings and floors because of the wear and tear it causes on the body. These types of jobs will go slower simply because they are more labor intensive.

Another scenario to charge more for is excess heights. Any time you have to work from planks, scaffolds or ladders extended beyond 8' (2.4m), you should charge extra. Not only will these types of jobs take longer, but they are more stressful than working at regular heights. Never accept a job where the conditions are unsafe, or if you do not have the appropriate equipment to complete the job safely.

When figuring your pricing, decide if you are going to charge for your initial consultation. Although I do not charge for the initial consultation, I know many decorative painters who weed out the "shoppers" by charging for this consultation. Usually the fee is nominal, and often it is refundable when the job is booked or is credited on the invoice.

Never lower your price. If the proposed bid is higher than the client wishes to pay, suggest a simpler painting procedure rather than meekly lowering your price to meet the budget or, if you really want the job and are willing to paint it for less, make the client think you are painting a simpler technique or design.

Consider how many samples you will do for the client before charging for them. There will always be clients who are indecisive and want to see the finished product in umpteen various colors or techniques. You can head this off at the pass by charging for excess sample boards. Since I feel I have to do a sample board for the client regardless, I do not charge for boards unless the client wants more than three. Decide what works best for you. You may decide you need to charge up front for each sample board you make, or you may feel no need to charge for sample-making time if you look on the exercise as practice time.

Referral Fees

A referral fee, a prearranged percentage amount added to the job price, is paid to anyone—interior designers, contractors or other professionals—who refers you to a potential job. This fee is usually 10 to 20 percent of the job price. Of course, you won't pay a referral fee if you do not book the job, but if the referral leads to a booking, pay this fee willingly, on good faith, because you would not have gotten the lead or the job without the referral. There need not be a big mystery surrounding referral fees; discuss this with the person when they are giving you the lead: "Thank you for the referral. What percentage would you like me to add to the job for your referral fee?" Sometimes you will get lucky and they'll want nothing, but if they should want more than 20 percent you should counter, "I normally pay 20 percent, would that be acceptable?" Some negotiation may be required, but keep in mind how much business you could earn from this particular referral source.

Charging Friends and Family

Working for friends and family can be awkward if you are not up front about your expectations right off the mark. When you are trying to gain

If the market will bear more than a 20 percent surcharge for a referral fee, your prices are too low for your market.

experience, you will want to impose your talents upon all unsuspecting friends and family members. However, after you begin to establish yourself in business, you will want to reaffirm to your friends and family that you are now in business and no longer just playing with your hobby.

I have found it helpful to establish (to quote the folks at Sprint) a "Friends and Family Rate." For me, this is a flat 25 percent discount from the total bill. Of course, there will always be family that you wouldn't charge for your services (you can't charge your own mother, can you?), or perhaps you could barter favors (i.e., stencil your brother's apartment in exchange for him working on your car), but drawing that line in the sand does much to establish your credibility as a professional among the people who matter to you most.

Summary

1. Pricing is an intensely personal subject. Only you can determine what your decorative painting services are worth.
2. Keep a written log of all time you spend working to help you track your nonbillable time. Record the time involved in making samples to use for estimating the job price.
3. Figure your billing rate by determining the number of hours in your workday, the number of work days in your workweek and the number of weeks per year that will constitute your actual working time. These figures will be used in the mathematical equations to determine your billing rate.
4. Do some detective work to figure out what the market will bear in

---

There will always be times when you do not get the job, even after you have spent time and energy bidding on it. Although this is disappointing, be gracious. Try to view it as a learning experience. The sample boards can be added to your portfolio, and you can chalk the rest up to experience.

your particular community and area of the country.

5. If you are getting every job you bid on, your prices are too low.

6. There are three methods of quoting a job price: by the job, by measurement and by time and materials.

7. Tack on a percentage to every job that qualifies for the "pain-in-the-rear factor."

8. Don't forget to add a percentage to your bill to cover referral fees.

9. Give friends and family a discount, but don't work for free.

Chapter 6

The Initial Consultation

Your networking has paid off and at last the telephone rings. The euphoria of having your first client call quickly begins to fade when you realize that you now have to perform.

The Initial Phone Contact

Make the most of the initial phone conversation by listening carefully and remembering to ask a few basic questions.

1. What does the client have in mind?

Listen carefully to the descriptive adjectives the client uses to describe what she would like you to paint for her. Understanding the client's desires now will be very important in determining how you will go about the job. If the client says, "I want something soft and subtle with very little color," you know immediately that the client does not want something bold and dramatic. If the client says he wants "something that will knock my neighbor's socks off," you have another clue, and you'd better start thinking big. Be sure to write down these clues.

2. When can we schedule an appointment so I can show you my portfolio?

In a perfect world, you have your business cards printed, your portfolio assembled, sample boards that will dazzle the clients and you are full of confidence. Okay, so perhaps not all your ducks are neatly in a row just yet. Don't panic! Tell the client you are booked up for the next few days, and then scurry and prepare for the appointment.

Try to schedule the appointment during daylight hours. This can be difficult when working around everyone's schedules, but seeing the room in natural light, seeing the fabric-swatch colors in natural light and not being tired will help make the consultation more effective.

3. How do I find you?

Get explicit directions so that you don't get lost going to the initial consultation. Write everything down, and clarify anything you are unsure about. Get a complete address, including ZIP code (which you will need for mailing the estimate), the correct spelling of the client's name and the phone numbers where the client can be reached should you have to change the appointment time.

Be sure to note the appointment on your master calendar and your smaller calendar.

4. How did you hear about me?

Note to yourself which of your marketing strategies paid off. Very often a prospective customer will tell you flat out, "I saw your ad in the *Daily Bugle*" or "I saw what you painted in Betty's house, and I would like something like that in my house." Be sure to keep track of effective marketing results for future reference.

Preparing for the Appointment

Presentation is everything. During the initial telephone contact you should have developed a strong feel for what interests the client. Do your

Never quote a price over the phone without seeing the job site.

homework. Make a sample board, if you do not already have something suitable, that in your mind best fits the client's description. I have often flagged pages in books, marked stencil patterns in catalogs or dug out appropriate sample boards to bring to the client.

Of course, this assumes the client has an idea of what they are looking for in mind. Often the client has no clue, knowing only that she wants *something.* For this presentation you will need to make a hodgepodge presentation of some, if not all, of the painting options. With clients of this type, it is a good idea to get a feel for their budget constraints before you offer them the world. It is very disappointing for you and for the clients to oversell them on something that isn't within their budget.

Get a Briefcase

You will need a case to contain and carry your estimating tools. Although you may not need a leather briefcase, I have found that having a case that latches shut is very important to avoid dumping my paperwork all over my client's driveway.

In this briefcase you will need to have your business cards, writing paper for making notes and room diagrams, pens and pencils, paint chip fan decks for color selection and matching, a binder full of stencil catalogs, a tape measure, your client's file folder and your calendar.

Dress for Success

Dressing for the appointment should not be a stressful event; however, being neat and tidy is important. Remember, not only are you selling your work, you are selling yourself. Even though this is a business appointment, you are an artist and, as such, are not required to wear a business suit (thank goodness!).

Listen to the clients' reactions for more clues about the types of painting that appeal to them. This is the key to zeroing in on what will satisfy your clients.

Meeting With the Client

Prepare as much ahead of time as possible. Be sure to take your portfolio, the directions to the client's house, any appropriate idea concepts you have gathered and your briefcase.

I have found that some clients want to monopolize your time and would have you spend the entire day with them discussing their project, or would like you to help them decorate their house. The following are suggestions to help you cut to the chase and keep the appointment on target.

1. *Be on time.* If for any reason you are going to be delayed, call the client. Better yet, allow yourself enough time so that this is not necessary. Better to drive around the block a few times than to be late!

2. *Plan on spending no more than one hour with the client.* Sometimes it's helpful to say right off the bat, "I have another appointment at 2:00," as that deadline will help you and the client keep to the task at hand. I have had clients pick my brains about things that have nothing to do with decorative painting, such as "Do these pillows really match the couch?"

3. *View the room first.* That way you can visualize what the client is talking about and plan a design concept more accurately. Take note of the decorating style and fabrics used in the room, or ask for swatches if the fabrics to be used are not available. This is important for style and color matching.

4. *Present your portfolio and samples.* Walk the client through your presentation. Explain to him what he is seeing. Be upbeat and confident about your work.

5. *Take accurate measurements of all room dimensions, and diagram the room layout.* This information is necessary to calculate the estimate and to

"The Six P's of Preparation: Proper Preparation and Practice Prevent Poor Performance."

—ROBERT PIKE, CREATIVE TRAINING TECHNIQUES HANDBOOK

determine the amount of supplies you will need to complete the job.

Write down all measurements of the room and of all surfaces to be painted. If your client is interested in a stenciled border, it may appear necessary to measure only the linear footage where the border will run. However, I have found it helpful to also have the square footage of all wall surfaces handy in case I can sell the client on a glazed wall finish as well as the stenciled border. (Gently suggesting more alternatives to your client is a great way to increase the scope of the job.)

Diagram all window and door configurations in the room. I do not subtract the square footage from doors and windows in my estimate because I feel that taping these areas off or adjusting the stenciling around them takes longer than if they were simply wall space. However, knowing the amount you need to subtract for doors and windows is important in figuring your supply needs (for example, a room with lots of doors and windows will require less paint but more tape).

Do not give the client a price on the spot. Tell the client you need time to calculate the job accurately. This gives you time to think about all aspects of the job, to estimate your time more accurately by sample making and to figure out a materials estimate.

Tell the client you will get back to her within a few days, or by a set date, with an estimate for the job and when she can expect the completed sample boards. Be realistic and do not promise a deadline that you cannot meet. I usually prepare the estimate within 24 hours of the consultation and get it in the mail. I do not prepare sample boards until I hear the bid has been accepted, unless the client specifically requests boards to help make decisions. There is no point in spending time preparing samples if your work is not within the client's budget.

Be sure to leave your client feeling secure that you are the right person for the job. Good salesmanship can accomplish that, but knowing your craft can instill even more confidence. Be friendly and charming, and most of all believe in yourself, and that confidence will shine through.

Summary

1. Listen carefully during the initial telephone conversation with your prospective client. Write down what painting project he has in mind, where you will meet him and when.

2. Prepare for the appointment in advance by researching books and catalogs or preparing or gathering specific samples.

3. Purchase a briefcase in which to carry your consulting tools.

4. Dress for success by being neat, tidy and professional.

5. Keep the appointment on track by staying focused on the painting project.

6. Take accurate notes. Measure and diagram the room.

7. Do not give the client a price on the spot. Take the data back to your office to prepare the estimate, and mail it to the client as quickly as possible.

8. Leave your client feeling that you are the best person for the job!

Chapter 7

Proposals, Contracts and Letters of Agreement

P roposals, contracts and letters of agreement all accomplish one main objective: clarifying your intentions and expectations by putting it in writing. This helps to define and spell out, in everyone's mind, all objectives, rights and responsibilities of the parties involved.

No matter whether you choose to submit to your client a typed estimate (job proposal) specific to each commission, along with a simple a letter of agreement to be signed by all the parties involved, or an estimate included in a formal preprinted contract, these documents will help avoid any misunderstandings throughout the painting process. And, obviously, these documents will protect you and the client should any misunderstandings occur.

Putting It in Writing

The flavor of each of these documents is decidedly different. A proposal is a written estimate of the services the decorative painter intends to provide and how much those services will cost the client. A contract is often a stiff and formal agreement between the decorative painter and the client. Usually the contract is preprinted on a carbonless form. A letter of agreement is decidedly more informal, usually written on business letterhead, spelling out the basics of the job. You must decide which form works best with your style of business, or perhaps you want to develop your own document using a combination of all these forms. I decided to use all three documents in my business because I deal with my clients by listening to my gut instincts. If I suspect a client (or the client's spouse) is going to be a problem, I'll pull out my full-fledged, most fine-printed-legalese contract. I also use this contract for all commercial work I do. For the simpler, friendlier jobs, I use a letter of agreement that simply states the terms of the job and how much I expect to be paid for the privilege of working with the client.

Proposals

The proposal, or the formal estimate form, is a written statement of intent by the decorative painter. The proposal should clearly state a detailed description of all work to be performed, an estimate of all costs, the number of samples to be provided to the client, any preparation work necessary, the expected payment schedule, an expiration date for when the proposal expires and a method for agreement between the parties.

The proposal should be neatly typewritten on business letterhead. Prepare an extra copy to keep in your client file. The proposal should include the following elements.

1. The Job Description

Specify all surfaces to be painted or excluded from painting. This will help clarify the painting process for all parties involved. This is not the time to be vague. For example, instead of saying "Glaze Bedroom," you should state: Rose-color (paint chip #123) alkyd glaze, parchment finish, to be applied to all master bedroom walls (650 sq. ft.), excluding soffit areas and ceiling, as shown on sample board provided.

Taking the time to painstakingly prepare a full job description will also help clarify and plan each step of the painting process necessary to complete the job.

2. Estimated Fees and Costs

I suggest the client should be presented with only the estimated total cost for completing the job, no matter how you figure your estimate. This prevents haggling over the estimated price. Be sure to use the word *estimate*, as this term will allow a reasonable change in price, either more or less.

I charge separately for labor and materials, so I give the client a separate cost breakdown for materials, or I include the phrase ''all materials to be billed separately from the above labor estimate.'' However, you may prefer to include the cost of materials in the total estimated job price. The act of itemizing the materials will help to define in your mind what materials and supplies will be necessary to complete the project.

3. The Number of Samples

Spell out exactly how many samples you are going to complete for this particular job. If you are doing several different applications, of course you will provide more than one sample. However, if you are only going to execute a simple wall finish, one or two samples is reasonable. Instruct the client to sign the back of the sample board to constitute approval and acceptance of the sample provided.

4. Preparation of the Work Surfaces

If the client is responsible for the preparation work and base coat colors, this should be spelled out clearly in the proposal, noting the sheen of the paint to be used as well as the brand and color: Client is to have all applicable wall surfaces patched, primed and base-coated in eggshell latex finish, Color #234. If the decorative painter is to perform the prep work, this should also be spelled out step by step on the proposal form.

5. Payment Schedule

You must determine what type of payment schedule suits your business needs. Some decorative painters require only a minimal deposit, with the balance due on completion. Others require a deposit to calendar a start date, another amount before work starts and the balance on completion.

Some decorative painters charge nothing until the work is completed. But taking a deposit will help you avoid the waffling client who may change his mind at the last minute. Like pricing, your payment method will be highly individualized and must suit your own needs and expectations.

6. Expiration Date

The proposal should contain an expiration date (this estimate valid for 90 days). You will not want to have a client call you a year later, after you have reevaluated your pricing structure, and demand that you do the job as proposed a year earlier.

7. Terms of Agreement

Assuming the proposal is acceptable to the client, the next step would be to finalize the acceptance with a contract or letter of agreement, or, if it suits your style, you could simply have the client sign a copy of the proposal and return it to you along with the deposit.

Letters of Agreement

The letter of agreement is a document, customized for each individual commission, stating that the terms and conditions outlined in the proposal are acceptable to all parties. The letter can be informal and still state the terms and conditions in a business-like manner. The client signs off on the letter of agreement to accept the terms and conditions as stated, and returns the letter to the decorative painter along with a deposit.

Contracts

A contract is a standardized document drawn up by the decorative painter stating the terms and conditions applicable to the decorative painting process. The contract is a more rigid form, and thus is worded less specifically in terms of an individual job. Using standardized language to spell out the terms and conditions applicable to any given job, your contract should clearly state the roles of the parties involved, the expectations of those parties and the consequences if those expectations are not met.

Terms and Conditions

Whether you choose to use a customized letter of agreement or a standardized contract, each document must contain terms and conditions set forth by the decorative painter. Clearly stating these terms will help eliminate any confusion as to responsibility and accountability of both the decorative painter and the client. Basically, the document should include the following terms.

1. The terms of the proposal are accepted as stated, and the proposal is now considered part of these terms and conditions. In other words, the client accepts the proposal as written.

2. The client shall be responsible for removing all window treatments, works of art and valuables from the painting area. The client shall also see that all furniture is moved at least 3′ (0.9m) away from the walls to provide the decorative painter free access to the wall.

3. The room shall be ready (all prep work completed) by the calendared start date. Forty-eight hours notice of any delay shall be given to the decorative painter. If notice is not given, a penalty of $X shall be assessed for each day work stoppage occurs (usually an amount equal to one or two days of your daily billing rate). The decorative painter accepts no responsibility for the quality of work provided by other tradespeople.

4. Price of materials is subject to change without notice. Any change in the price of labor shall be made only by agreement of both parties. Changes to the design shall result in an additional fee approved by both parties before changes are implemented.

5. The decorative painter is, within reason, entitled to use creative license in the execution of the project. It is understood that samples are representative of the proposed application, and the actual results may differ slightly.

6. The decorative painter reserves the right to photograph all work.

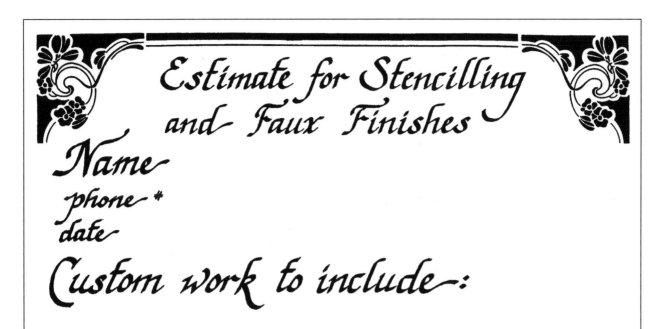

Estimate for Stencilling and Faux Finishes

Name

phone #

date

Custom work to include:

Date work will be started:

Customer's signature:_____

Stenciller's signature:_____

Terms: ⅓ payment when contract is signed, balance due upon completion of work. Requests for changes in design may require changes in estimate.

P.J. Tetreault ~ 438-8020

43 Lockrow Blvd.

Albany, N.Y. 12205

Sample estimate

North Shore Wall Design

D E C O R A T I V E   P A I N T I N G

1023 Oakwood Avenue — Wilmette, Illinois 60091
Phone (847) 853-0904

Estimate

Mrs. Martha Howard   May 23, 1997
24 Main Street
Winnetka, IL 60093

Nursery Painting:
Bears dancing around maypole, copied from nursery fabric, approximately 24″ tall,
painted on wall above crib.
Colors and style to match fabric sample provided.

Simple balloon border stenciled at chairrail height around room (approximately 36″
from floor). Colors and style to match fabric sample provided. Border not to be stenciled on crib wall.

Estimated Labor:	$550.00
Estimated Materials, Stencil Cutting & Design:	$80.00
TOTAL ESTIMATE FOR NURSERY PAINTING	$630.00

An estimate for decorative painting

DECORATIVE ACCENTS
BY
PEGGY EISENBERG

June 9, 1997

Mrs. Martha Brown
380 Vancouver Lane
Woodstone, CA 94099

Dear Mrs. Brown:

I hereby submit specifications and proposal for the hand painting of a
garden mural in you master bathroom:

GLAZES

MARBLE

STENCIL   Hand painting of garden mural on three walls of master bathrrom in bath
                 tub and shower area: $2300.00
MURALS

TROMPE L'OEIL
                 Line drawing to be approved prior to commencement.

                 Payment terms: Deposit of one half due upon acceptance of proposal.
                 Remainder due upon completion.

                 All work to be completed in a workmanlike manner according to standard
                 practices. Any alteration or deviation from specifications involving extra
                 cost will be executed upon written orders and will become an extra charge
                 over and above the quotation.

                                          DECORATIVE ACCENTS
                                          DESIGN STUDIO

                                          By_____
                                          Peggy Eisenberg

                                                    111 Comstock Road
                                          Woodside, California 94062-4507
                                                        (415) 851-7110

                                                    License No. 645488

A letter of agreement. Used with permission by Peggy Eisenberg, *Decorative Accents Design Studio*

Artistic Stencils

Decorative Interior Painting
Stenciling and Faux Finishing

Claudia Stahl
1990 E. Oakshire Circle
Sandy, UT 84092
(801) 576-9660

PROPOSAL AND ACCEPTANCE

PROPOSAL SUBMITTED FOR:

Phone Number _____

Commencement Date: _____

Todays Date: _____

Project Description:

Payment Terms and Conditions

For the sum of $, I agree to the above project description. A 50% payment is due upon signing of the contract, balance is due upon completion. **NOTE:** *Any additional work required will be subject to a separate contract and bid to be approved by client prior to commencement of work, payment terms as above.* If client fails to pay the remaining balance within 30 days of completion of the job, an 18% annual interest charge will accrue on unpaid balance. This proposal is valid for 60 days from the above date and may require a new bid if not accepted within this time.

Artistic Stencils will supply up to 4 sample boards in the clients choice of colors for the non-refundable fee of $50.00. This fee shall be paid at time of consultation. Client will approve sample boards prior to commencement of work. Sample boards and/or stencils shall remain the property of *Artistic Stencils.*

Client agrees to remove all nails, switch plates, drapery rods, pictures, decorations or other obstructions prior to commencement of work. Walls must be in good repair, without holes, dents, mars or nail holes. All furniture must be moved at least 3 feet from wall to allow enough room to maneuver equipment and ladders and should be covered for protection. If room is not prepared to the above mentioned specifications by commencement date and/or other arrangements have not been made between client and artist prior to that date, a $50.00 charge will be added to the proposal.

Artistic Stencils shall guarantee work to be in accordance with sample boards.   Work such as plastering, base coating and finishing done by tradespeople hired directly by client or designer, or walls subjected to damage and/or abuse, is not the responsibility of *Artistic Stencils.*

I have read this contract and agree to its contents.

_____   _____
Client   Date

_____   _____
Artist   Date

A decorative painting contract. Used with permission by Claudia Stahl, *Artistic Stencils*

7. Cancellation that occurs well in advance of a start date should require the decorative painter to refund a portion of the deposit, excluding the amount of deposit used for sample-making time and materials purchased. Some decorative painters state in their proposals that all deposits are nonrefundable.

8. The document should have a place for the date and the signatures of all parties.

No matter what vehicle you choose to obtain your client's acceptance of your terms for completing the job, always submit two copies to the client. Have the client sign both—she will keep a copy and return the other one to you. A good time to collect your deposit is along with the accepted bid. Ideally, all contracts should be signed before any work, even sample making, starts.

I know several decorative painters who do not use contracts in their business. These individuals operate on the blind faith that the world will treat them fairly: They honor their word and the word of their clients. While I cannot in clear conscience recommend this practice, obviously this method of operation has worked in their businesses, or they would need a written contract. Trust your instincts, but don't trust your luck too long. Developing a contract you are comfortable with can protect you and spare you endless grief.

Summary

1. A proposal, or written estimate, should include:
    a. a clear description of all work to be performed
    b. an estimate of all costs
    c. the number of samples to be provided to the client
    d. the preparation work necessary and who is responsible for its completion

Job Proposal #1

Date: August 24, 1997
For: [CLIENT NAME]
      [CLIENT ADDRESS]
      [CLIENT PHONE #]

I am pleased to present this proposal for custom decorative artwork as described below:

Area #1—[DESCRIBE WORK TO BE DONE IN DETAIL, INCLUDING STENCIL DESIGN # IF APPLICABLE]

Cost—XXXX
Exact placement to be decided by mutual agreement of stenciler and client, with input from Interior Decorator. Price includes all taping of doors, windows, ceilings, adjacent walls; all materials, supplies, disposables, further consultations and equipment to complete artwork as described above. Drop cloths will be used on all flooring beneath work area. If new base coating of walls is to be done before stenciling, it is the responsibility of the client and should be a *latex eggshell finish.*

Work schedule/Payment terms:
A color sample (one complete repeat of each stencil, in desired color combinations) on clear mylar will be rendered at a *non-refundable* charge of XXXX [THIS CHARGE COVERS MY TIME AND MATERIALS IN MAKING THE COLOR SAMPLE]. If by mutual agreement of the stenciler and client the proposed job will *not* be executed after rendering of color sample, the balance of the proposal becomes null and void. All materials, supplies, and samples will remain the property of [ARTIST]. If color samples are approved and work is to continue, the color sample fee will serve as job deposit [THIS IS GENERALLY FOR JOBS UNDER $500; IF A LARGER JOB, ½ OF JOB ESTIMATE IS DUE—ARTIST'S DISCRETION]. When work is completed, the balance of the job cost XXXX is due and payable.

Any changes to the original proposal must be agreed upon in writing by the artist and client, and may affect the total cost of the job. Feel free to call to discuss any parts of the above proposal. Scheduling of job will be by mutual agreement of the client and [ARTIST]. Regular workdays are, [DAYS/TIME DURING EACH DAY], as mutually agreed upon.

To accept proposal as written, please sign on appropriate line on second page and return to [ARTIST] with color sample payment. Please make checks payable to ''[ARTIST].''

This quotation is good for 60 days from above date

I agree to the proposal as written and understand the terms and conditions.

_____
Client signature & date

Offered by:

[ARTIST'S SIGNATURE] _____
for [COMPANY NAME]

For later use:

Colors: _____
_____

A proposal
Used with permission by Carole Haines Shearer, *Stenciling, Etc.*

     e. the expected payment schedule

     f. an expiration date

     g. the method of acceptance of the terms of the proposal

2. A letter of agreement is a letter written on business letterhead stating the specific terms of the proposal are acceptable to all parties.

3. A contract is a more formal, preprinted document stating the general terms and conditions of the decorative painter.

4. Choose a method of putting it in writing that suits your business and your personal style.

Chapter 8

Sample Making

Taking the time to prepare a sample board, using the exact same steps, colors and techniques to be used in the final application, is a very important step in the total decorative painting process. No decorative technique should be applied to the wall, a piece of furniture or any other surface without making a sample board first. Without a sample board, you have no way of affirming that the design concept will indeed work, which is why a sample is often called a "painted proof."

A sample board is another tool to allow you visual affirmation that you truly understand your client's wishes. It is common practice to have the client sign the back of the sample board to indicate approval of the colors and techniques. Your proposal form should confirm that the client signature constitutes approval.

And unless you do a trial run of the paint techniques involved, you are shooting in the dark when it comes to pricing the work.

Using Index Cards

When sample making, be sure to write down on an index card all the colors, techniques and painting steps involved in the project. If you are using standardized colors (i.e., bottled acrylic colors or a custom-mixed wall paint), be sure to write down the specific product name, as well as the color name and number. I have found it helpful to include dollops of each color on the index card as a reference. The index card can then be placed in the client file (after it's dry, of course). You may want to transfer the color names and numbers to the back of the sample board after the board has dried. Of course, if you are worried about someone copying your sample, you will not want to write your color choices and techniques on the back of the sample. But I have found it useful to have these reference points on the samples I use in my portfolio to explain various painting processes and to answer the client's questions. At the very least, mark the board with the client's name as a cross reference, so you can refer to the card in the client file for the painting procedure.

The Mechanics of Creating a Sample

If you are making several samples at a time, you should label the index card so it correlates to the correct sample board. This could be something simple like "Smith Sample #1." Again, you think you won't get the samples mixed up—but trust me, it's very easy to do.

The finished sample board should be placed somewhere clean, dry and dust free while it dries. Nothing is more disheartening than to have something mar a perfect sample. And if you are like me, you probably do not have enough time to repaint the sample before the date the board was promised to the client. Allowing the board to dry in a room where the temperature and humidity are nearly equal to the job site will also give you data on the drying times should you need this information for multi-step processes.

Samples can be painted on lots of different types of boards or papers. I use artist's mat boards for wall glazing or faux finishing samples because they stay flat when wet, and look very professional when dry. Stenciling or other painted samples can be done on blank-stock wallpaper, which can be purchased at your local home center. This paper can be unrolled to any length to accommodate the length of the stencil design. The finish on blank-stock wallpaper is often similar in texture to the walls, which provides an accurate texture to stencil on, unlike regular paper. If the client requires a larger sample of a faux technique, blank-stock wallpaper works well for wall finishes, too. Poster board makes an economical sample board. Watercolor paper works well for mural sketches, with washes of color added to bring the sketch to life. Samples can be also be painted effectively on sailcloth or cambric cloth, which rolls up nicely for shipping or storage. If a sturdy and indestructible sample is required, I suggest using styrene plastic. Samples that are going to be handled often, like your portfolio samples, can be laminated to protect them from dirt and grime. Samples for furniture finishes or painted moldings can be painted on small pieces of wood, wood trim or Masonite. These pieces can then be drilled with a small hole and ringed together.

Always base coat the sample board with the same paint that will be used on the project. The base-coat paint always affects the success of the decorative paint treatment: For example, if the decorative paint soaks into the base coat too quickly, there is not enough time to manipulate and work the paint. The base-coat paint will also affect how the colors react and play off each other: The color may be perfect on a white background, but appear muddy and dull on a beige background.

When you are making a sample of a wall glaze or a faux finish and will be painting the entire board, be sure to tape off one corner of the board so that it will remain unpainted, showing the base-coat color. This area shows the client (and reminds you of) the base-coat color needed to achieve the end result. And having a corner taped off also gives you somewhere to place your fingers while you paint the board.

Unless you are doing samples for your portfolio, do not "frame" the entire board (tape all the edges off) because the paint treatment should reach all the way to the edges of the sample board. By bringing the paint technique all the way to the edges of the board, your client can see how the application looks against his fabrics and moldings without the distraction of a flat-color or white frame around the board. However, if you are making faux finish samples for your portfolio, having this neat and tidy frame around the sample gives you a professional-looking board. Should the tape leak, be sure to tidy up the edges while the paint is still wet.

It is much harder to prepare a sample, or proof, for murals. While some people are satisfied with the idea of turning the artist loose, most clients need something more concrete to help them visualize the end result, and to instill confidence that you have the skill necessary to complete the project satisfactorily. I prepare a rough sketch, a working drawing, of the mural, often adding a wash of color to give it some life. I provide a color palette of the colors I will use in the mural for the client to approve. And if the client still requires more input, I will paint one element of the mural. This gives the client a better idea of my painting style without recreating the whole mural.

Unless you want to provide the client with endless samples to choose from, you should specify a finite number of samples you will provide for final selection. Because not everyone can make up their mind from a choice of only one or two sample boards, you can establish an excess sample fee (which for me is more than three samples). This will help curtail the client who wants to see the sample in fifteen different textures or colors. While sample making is a very important part of the decorative painting process, it is unbillable time and should be kept to a minimum.

Be sure to retain possession of your sample boards. Although I will leave a sample board with a client to "live with" for a limited amount of time, I always ask for the sample boards back. Sometimes a client needs to show the work to a significant other, or perhaps wants to study the finish in different lights (night vs. day). This is reasonable. Keeping a board while shopping the competition is not. If at the end of the job the client wants the sample board for decorating purposes, I will offer her a portion of the board, or simply make a palette sheet of the colors for reference. The boards are great for future reference and are necessary for building your portfolio; at the very least, they can be recycled and repainted for the next client. Be sure to keep your sample boards.

Always remember that working on a sample board is far easier than working on a wall. You won't be doing yourself, or your client, any favors if you create a sample that looks smashing on the board but is impossible to re-create as a final product.

Sample vs. Reality

What do you do when, despite your best efforts, you begin the project and realize that the paint you are applying does not match the sample board? This is every decorative painter's nightmare and, unfortunately, it isn't all that uncommon. We are not machines capable of reproducing replicas time after time. Sometimes dye lots of the paint are different. Sometimes the base coat you are painting on isn't what you specified. Sometimes the weather affects the paint's performance. But what do you do? You have several options.

First, if the disparity is vastly different, you need to stop immediately. Do not finish the entire room and hope the client won't notice. If you haven't gotten very far, remove as much of the paint as possible. Hopefully you will have the base-coat paint handy if the decorative paint cannot be removed with solvent. Assess the situation, find the solution and begin again after solving the problem.

However, if the colors seem to work in the room setting, and you find you are very close to the sample, consider it artistic license to continue. You can remove the sample from the job site, and hopefully no one will be the wiser. But this gamble comes at a price. If the client notices the disparity, you will be at his mercy to correct the problem or, at the very least, to explain the discrepancy, which can be embarrassing.

"Working with paint is like raising children: You never know how either are going to behave."

—BARBARA WAGNER

In both of these scenarios, I suggest calling the client in and telling him you would like him to see the painting before you continue. This doesn't mean running out of the room with your hair on fire, all in a dither. It will be up to you how much of a problem you want to admit to the client, and you certainly won't want to point out a discrepancy. Asking the client to view the work in progress isn't admitting a problem, and it is often a good idea even if the sample matches exactly. Never try to bluff your way around a problem because your credibility and business reputation are at stake.

One solution to avoid this type of problem was suggested by a decorative painting friend of mine. She suggests having a spare sample board base-coated and ready when you start the job to test your colors and technique on. This gives you a place to adjust your colors or the thickness of the paint or glaze without having to test your materials directly on the wall or project surface.

Weather affects paints and wall glazes. If the humidity is extremely high or low, it will affect the drying time and how much time you have to manipulate the paint. You could postpone the job until the weather is a bit more temperate, or try to adjust the humidity levels by using fans, humidifiers or dehumidifiers. In time you will learn how to make the paint cooperate in most conditions, but there will be times (like those extreme days we often have here in Chicago) that you simply cannot force the paint to perform and consequently must reschedule the job.

Another factor in variation from the sample to the job application might simply be *you*. We are not robots who can crank out exactly the same results time after time. I have found that my painting style varies from day to day. I can be heavy-handed one day, light and timid the next. Over a period of time you learn to recognize when you need to lighten up or beef it up, depending on your stamina or mood.

Your sample boards will be a testimony to your painting style and your business philosophy. Never show a client a messy sample board! This attention to detail instills confidence in your clients and will speak volumes about your business ethics.

Summary

1. When painting a sample, keep a record of all colors and techniques used. I am always amazed at how quickly the memory fades, usually faster than the board dries, and if I do not write everything down, I am left wondering, "How did I do that?"

2. Use an index card for making notes on your sample-making techniques, colors and time factors. Be sure to place a dollop of all paints and glazes you use on the sample on an index card for future reference, and place the card in the client file. If you are painting with premixed colors, be sure to note the paint name and dye lot number on the card, too.

3. Samples can be made on lots of different types of papers and boards. Choose a surface that works best for the project at hand. Take into account transportation considerations, mailing (lightweight vs. cumbersome; rollable vs. nonpliant surfaces) and durability (does it need to hold up to repeated handling) when choosing a sample-making medium.

4. Always base-coat your sample in the same paint that will be used in the final application.

5. Give your client a finite number of samples from which to choose the particular application. Have your client show approval by signing and dating the back of the sample.

6. Always maintain physical control of your painted sample boards.

7. Do not create a sample so intricate it cannot be reproduced in the final application.

8. Do not try to bluff your way around the problem if a painted sample does not match the final application. Take steps to correct the problem immediately.

Chapter 9

Managing the Job Site

All the time and energy invested in planning your business and all the preparation work has been geared for this moment—a chance to put paint on the walls (or whatever the particular application) and get paid for the privilege. It is exciting and nerve-wracking all at the same time. It's "put up or shut up" time. Even after all these years of painting, I am still nervous before I start a job. I usually don't sleep well and, when I finally do sleep, my dreams are filled with painting scenarios. Doing your homework and being as prepared for all contingencies as much as humanly possible will do much to lower your stress level.

Highlighting the particular supplies you will need on the supply lists mentioned previously (see page 40) will eliminate the possibility of forgetting to pack an important supply. Having your supplies organized in convenient storage bins helps you load your painting supplies quickly and efficiently. I find that taking the time to gather all my supplies and equipment the night before greatly helps reduce my fitful sleep and painting dreams.

Be sure to allow yourself enough time. Being late will only add unnecessary stress to the start of a job.

After you greet the client, check to see that the room is in the appropriate condition for you to begin work. The walls should be clean and ready to go, the furniture moved, the pets locked up, the small children bound and gagged and the coffee freshly brewed. Ah, such would be a perfect world! But instead, as is often the case, the client has already left for work, the base coat painting is done but marginal at best, the furniture and furnishings are everywhere, the dog is barking and the cat is eyeing you from the middle of the homeowner's bed, which hasn't been moved away from the wall. You hunt down the base-coat paint, with the dog in hot pursuit, so you can touch up what the painters missed. As you begin to tape, you realize that cat hair is making the tape less tacky than it must be to stick to the wall. As you trip over the chair left in your way for the second time, you realize you need to revise your contract once again, because obviously no one is reading the part about moving the furniture away from the work area. At this point, accept that you have two choices: You could be a prima donna and walk away from the job site until your conditions are met, or you could put the dog outside, readjust the furniture to give you a bit more room, lock the cat in the laundry room with his litter box, use your Dust Buster to clean up the pet hair, touch up the paint where it's necessary and begin to work. Believe me, the client will be much happier with the second scenario than he will be with the first.

Setting Up

As you enter the job setting, lay down a tarp or an old towel to hold your painting supplies. Even though you know your paint supplies are clean and dry, most of the time it looks like they're going to leave a mess. It is the first step you can take to reassure your client that you will be neat and tidy. Unload everything you will need from your car at one time. If the homeowner has to contain pets and children, it's best they only have to do so for a short period of time. Remove your shoes if it's muddy outside; if the client is particularly fastidious, remove your shoes regardless of the weather. On mucky weather days, it's a good idea to bring a spare pair of clean and dry shoes to wear in the client's house.

Move any furniture and breakables that the homeowner forgot to clear out of your way. Ideally, this should have been done for you, but I am always amazed at the number of people who leave family heirlooms in the painter's path.

Tape off all areas that are to remain unpainted. If you are painting a stencil border, you won't need to tape off much, but if you are applying a wall glaze, you will need to tape off baseboards, windows, doors, the ceiling and the trim that are not to be glazed. Taping off baseboards and ceilings in a crisp straight line is the sign of a professional decorative painter, so check the accuracy of your tape, being sure it forms a crisp, straight line before you begin to paint. It is much easier to correct the straight line by adjusting the tape before you paint than it is to straighten the edges by repairing the line with paint or solvent afterwards. It is also a good idea to tape off adjacent walls so you can squeeze paint into the corners without smudging. Painting corners is another mark of a professional—try not to make them too heavy or leave light spots where little or no paint gets into the corners.

Remove all switch plates and outlet covers. Place the screws back into the holes so they do not get lost. Be sure to paint these plates (if they are to be painted) in the base color so they will disappear on the wall rather than become the focal point. One decorative painter I know takes these plates home, sprays them with an all-purpose sealer/primer, base-coat paints them and glazes them—at no extra charge! Needless to say, she has a large and happy client base. Be sure to tape off the actual switches and outlets so they will stay clean.

Spread tarps over all floor areas, and plastic over all furniture left in the room. Be sure you have enough tarps to cover the entire floor and overlap each other, in case the tarps slip while you are walking around on them. Nothing cuts into the profit margin more than paint that goes astray.

Set up your work area so that all the tools you will need are handy but not in your way. Put away all the tape and other tools you are finished with once the prep work is done. Often the actual preparation of a job site, such as preparing a room for wall glazing, takes as long as painting the walls. Be sure to note how long the process actually takes you, and chart it on your time log.

Prepare your paint palette, mix your glaze, test your colors and dig in. Putting the first swipe of color on the wall is always the hardest part of the job. Take a deep breath and exhale (loudly if the client isn't standing there watching you). It's always a good idea to start in the least conspicuous corner or part of the room (behind a large piece of furniture or a bed). If you are stenciling a border and want to be sure the main part of the pattern is centered over a window, or centered on a predominant wall, be sure to start there and work in opposing directions from that focal point into the least conspicuous corner (behind the door) of the room.

Painting

It's at this point that my grade school teacher's favorite admonishment comes to mind—"Neatness Counts!" Try to contain the mess and the paint as best you can.

1. *Keep your hands clean.* Do not touch anything without wiping off or cleaning your hands or removing your gloves. This includes a cup of coffee, the phone, the doorknob or even the faucets where you go to wash you hands.

2. *Keep cotton swabs in your apron pocket for small touchups,* and a wet paper towel draped across the back of the ladder for larger cleanups.

3. *Keep a trash bag handy.* Be very careful with wet tape and used palette sheets.

4. *Keep your paint bucket within a larger bucket to catch drips.* Be sure to put the drippy paint cans or bottles back into your carryall bin.

5. *Attach your palette to your ladder to keep it from spilling.*

6. *Keep your wet brushes in your apron pocket;* place dirty brushes you are finished with in a plastic bag for later cleaning. Falling or rolling brushes can leave a trail of destruction in their wake.

7. *Keep your path clear.* Don't put anything where you could trip over it,

and by no means put your paint anywhere near where you step off the ladder. The only time I ever accidentally got paint on a carpet was because I stepped on my wet sponge (left in my path) and had paint on my shoe without realizing it. When I walked out of the room, the paint came with me. Luckily I saw it quickly, and it came right up off the carpet.

8. *Wear gloves and an apron to protect your skin and clothes.*

Breaking the Monotony

Something happens after the first few repeats of a pattern, or midway through the first of four walls. You begin to realize that you have a long row to hoe. While the first hour or two of work seems to fly by, the third and fourth hours begin to get longer and longer. Just about the time you realize that what you are painting is becoming monotonous, you also begin to realize you have muscles and body parts you weren't aware you even owned. At this point you need to take a break. Finish the section you are working on and stop. Walk out of the room. Get something to eat and drink, and go outside for some fresh air. Five minutes will do wonders.

Another trick for relieving the monotony is to have fun, upbeat music to listen to, or a good book on tape. Of course you don't want to become so wrapped up in a song or story plot that you don't pay attention to your work, but there are times when you really don't need to think much while you're painting. Conversely, at other times your concentration level is so intense that any noise or distraction will be very annoying. That is also a sign that it could be time to take a small break to relieve the tension. Doing some stretching will help unkink your tired, knotted muscles. I'm also a big believer in taking ibuprofen as soon as the pain sets in. Taking an anti-inflammatory drug douses the fire in my muscles before they completely burst into flames.

Tear Down/Cleanup

When you are finished painting, complete a thorough check and double-check to make sure that everything is as it should be. All painted surfaces are evenly covered, the edges and corners are neat and crisp, the stencil pattern is straight, the colors are balanced and in harmony with other features of the room, and you have completed every part of the job as promised—in other words, you have done your best! At this point it would be appropriate to have the client take a look and give her final approval, if she is available. Once you have obtained the client's rave reviews, you can begin to clean up and tear down.

- Remove all tape carefully to avoid lifting the paint underneath. This means pulling the tape gently instead of ripping it off in one swoop from far away. Pulling the tape slowly also keeps it from marring the freshly painted wall finish. Fold the tape onto itself to contain the wet edges, and discard it in the trash bag you have nearby. Remove the trash to the cans outside or, if none are available, take the trash with you to dispose of later. Be sure to dispose of solvent-soaked rags properly.

- Check for leaks, drips and overspray that may have crept underneath or around the tape. Clean up all runs, drips and errors. Be sure to leave the unpainted surfaces as clean (or cleaner) than they were before you started the job.

- Fold all tarps onto themselves and take them outside to shake (if necessary).

"My business philosophy is basically to follow the Golden Rule: Treat others as you would like to be treated. This means showing up as close to the designated time as humanly possible, calling when problems or rescheduling needs arise, returning phone calls and treating clients (even if they tend to be a bit anal or downright stupid) with the same respect that I would want."

—Sharon A. Marriott

- Neatly label the leftover paint and leave it with the client. This way the paint is always available should any touchups be required later, and you will not be obligated to store it on the off chance the client may need it down the road. Having your business name preprinted on a sticky-type label to place on the paint can is a good advertising ploy and a pretty way to label the client's paint for him.

- Sweep up any debris left after the tarps are removed, polish the woodwork if the tape left it dull and put the furniture back the way you found it. Always leave the job site as clean or cleaner than you found it.

- If the client is not available when you are ready to leave, write a note asking her to call you when she returns. Leave extra business cards and your invoice.

- Should you have a job that takes more than one day to paint, you will need to ask your client what he would like you to do with your equipment at the end of the workday until the job can be completed. If you are lucky, the client will allow you to leave the work site set up and the door closed. However, it is still a good idea to clean the work area thoroughly at the end of your painting day.

- If you are not able to close off the work site, you should tear down your ladders, compile all your painting equipment in one location and cover it with a tarp. Fold all the remaining tarps so that no one trips over them.

Should the job site be in a high-traffic area (such as new construction) where many people will be coming and going while you are not there, do not leave your painting supplies, ladders, drop cloths or tools at the site. Unfortunately, these things have a way of disappearing or of being borrowed without permission. For your own peace of mind, it is worth it to tear down the work setup at the end of each day and redo it the next day.

The neater you can leave your work area at the end of each painting day, the nicer it will be for you to return to the next day, and it will leave your clients with the impression that you are fastidious and care about their homes as much as they do.

Summary

1. Use the master supply lists to highlight supplies you will need for your job.

2. Ideally, all furniture, bric-a-brac and family heirlooms will be removed from the job site before you begin, but if it isn't, be sure to move everything out of your way before you start setting up.

3. Tape off all areas that are not to be painted.

4. Remove switch plates and outlet covers to keep them clean, and tape off the actual switches and outlets so they don't get painted either.

5. Protect all floors with tarps, and cover all furniture remaining in the room with plastic sheeting.

6. When painting, the motto to remember is ''Neatness Counts!''

7. Take breaks when necessary, and listen to music to relieve the monotony.

8. Check to see that you have done everything to the absolute best of your ability before you begin to tear down your equipment and before you call the client in for her final approval.

9. Should your job require more than one painting day, ask the client how he would like you to store your supplies in the interim. To prevent theft or loss, do not leave your painting tools in a job site where there will be a lot traffic in and out of your painting area.

10. Be sure to leave your clients with the impression that you care as much about their homes or property as they do.

Chapter 10

Partnerships, Assistants and Employees

Painting can be a lonely business. Making creative decisions day in and day out, with no one to bounce your ideas off of, can add to your sense of isolation. When that blank wall, blank canvas or unpainted piece of furniture is staring back at you, painting does seem to be a lonely business indeed. And some aspects of decorative painting, such as applying a negative wall glaze, absolutely require more than one person, unless you are as fast as a one-armed paperhanger. In the long run, trying to do everything by yourself will take its toll on you. The physical demands of climbing ladders will wear you out, if the mental isolation doesn't wear you down first.

Having another person there to help you can alleviate the mental drain as well as the physical strain. Having a partner means sharing the responsibility for the business; having an employee means retaining control of the business but sharing the workload. Only you can ascertain the working relationship that will work best for you.

Partnerships

A good partnership is a gift. When personalities, painting styles and business styles mesh, a true partnership is formed. As rare as the possibility of that sounds, there are many wonderful examples of good partnerships in the decorative painting field.

The mechanics of the partnership will be as varied as any other personal relationship. One partner may be more business-minded and handle the office while the other is more of the *artiste*, or there may be an equal sharing of all aspects of the business. My partnership was a melding of our talents—what was a weak point in one partner was balanced by the other partner. We shared all decision making, client appointments, work and profits equally. We knew when to clear the air—before a grievance caused irreparable harm to our working relationship. And we had (and still have) enormous respect for each other. All those ingredients equaled a fantastic example of a good partnership. Sadly, our partnership ended when I moved from California to Chicago. To this day, we still refer to each other as ''my partner.''

Not all partnerships need be created equal. What about the decorative painter who has been established in business for a long time and decides to bring an assistant into the business as a partner? Or how about the partner who provides all the financing for the business? These partnership arrangements could be different from a 50/50 partnership. Not only would the profits be divided disproportionately, but so would the workload and responsibilities for the business.

Beware of the partnership where there is not an equal balance of power, however. Eventually both partners will feel that the situation is unfair (one will be working too hard, and the other will feel they aren't being paid enough), and it could cause trouble in the working relationship. Keep the lines of communication open, and be sure to discuss the direction of the business and the mechanics of the partnership often.

Partnership Agreements

Sitting down with your partner and spelling out (in writing) all your hopes, dreams and expectations, as well as your agreement on who is going to handle what and how each partner is going to be paid and how much, is a good exercise. This document need not be a formal partnership agreement (although you *could* have one drawn up if you feel the need), but it must be in writing and all parties must agree on its contents.

The following are topics for discussion and items to include in the agreement.

- How will client appointments be handled? By all partners, or will one partner act as "booking agent" for the business?
- Who's address and phone number will be used as the business office, or will you need office space?
- How will the purchase of business supplies be handled, and who will store the business supplies (stencils, paints, etc.)?
- Who will keep possession of the business assets should the partnership dissolve (or in my case, when one partner moves away)?
- Who will maintain the business checking account and business records?
- How will the partnership handle the tax situation?
- If one partner is totally responsible for the job lead, will that partner receive a finder's fee or an added percentage of the job's profit?
- Who will actually prepare the paperwork, such as estimates, contracts and billing?
- What contingency plans will you need if one person (or their kids) should get sick and can't work?

Assistants and Employees

I prefer to call my employee my "assistant." She means more to me than just hired help. But not all employees warrant the title assistant. A good assistant knows you and your working style and can accommodate you accordingly. Good assistants understand and accept your quirks—and are still willing to show up to work with you!

A good employee can make any job run smoother. Whether it's

someone to act as "gofer" or someone who applies paint to the wall, a second pair of hands will lighten your load. You may want to retain control over the painted finish, and have your employee execute everything else—setup, taping and cleanup. This alone can be a huge relief to the overwrought decorative painter.

One very successful decorative painter I know has two assistants and one hired helper. While she and her assistants get down to the business of painting, the helper sets up and tapes ahead of them, and then follows behind them doing the cleanup and tear down. Another decorative painter I know has such a good working relationship with her assistant that the assistant will assemble and load all the equipment into the van for each job because she is so familiar with the procedures. This allows the decorative painter time to return phone calls or work on sample boards.

Of course, the downside to this arrangement is that you will have to pay your assistant. Not all businesses have enough income to warrant an employee; conversely, not all businesses can survive without them. If you are only working intermittently on small jobs, you will not need an assistant. But should you decide to branch out and accept larger commissions, you will need an employee or assistant to help you complete jobs in a timely manner. You will also need an assistant if you are turning down work because you cannot calendar jobs in a timely manner, and are losing work because you are overbooked.

You can hire your assistant as an independent contractor or as an employee of the business. Hiring an independent contractor means that your assistant is not your employee, and as such, he is responsible for his own taxes and insurance. To protect yourself, it's a good idea to have the independent contractor (your assistant) provide you with a certificate of insurance before he begins to work with you, verifying that he does indeed have adequate coverage for all liabilities. At the end of the year you will provide your assistant, as an independent contractor, with Form 1099, showing the IRS that you have indeed paid income to this person.

If you choose to hire an assistant as an employee, you are responsible for withholding FICA and Social Security from the income you pay to the employee. This money is then held in a tax-escrow account and is paid to the IRS quarterly. Along with this payment, you will have to file quarterly employee tax returns. At the end of the year you will have to provide your employee with Form W-2 showing all earnings and withholdings. You, as the employer, will also need to provide insurance coverage for all your employees.

Whether you hire your assistant as an employee or as an independent contractor, you will have to determine the best method of paying your help for her time. Paying your assistant by the hour, rather than by the day or by the job, is fairer to both of you. If the job or the day runs longer or shorter, the employee will be compensated for her actual working time. Have your assistant keep a time log or time card and submit an invoice weekly.

When you make the decision to branch out, a hiring agreement must be negotiated before anyone goes to work for you. Even if you have a verbal agreement, it does not hurt to put your agreement in writing to avoid any misunderstandings further down the road. This agreement should include the following elements.

- *What are your expectations for your assistant?* Will she be painting right along side of you, or will she only do the preparation and cleanup of the job site? Will your assistant be expected to wash brushes or clean stencils?

- *What will your assistant be paid per hour?* Determine if you are going to pay for lunch breaks or travel time. Decide at what intervals you will pay your assistant (i.e., at the end of each job, once a week, bimonthly or monthly). Be sure to resolve the tax liability issues before issuing the first paycheck.

- *How many days per week/month will your assistant work?* Can she work flexible hours, or will she work a set time each day?

- *How are you going to handle the liability issues?* Be sure you have adequate insurance for all worst-case scenarios. As noted above, if you hire your assistant as an independent contractor, be sure that she provides you with a certificate of insurance.

- *Are you going to provide all the equipment* (ladders, brushes, gloves), or is your assistant expected to bring her own?
- *How will you travel to the job site?* Will your assistant come to your house and help you load equipment, or will she meet you at the job site?

Having another person on the job site can do wonders for your morale. It can reduce your job stress when you are forced to stop and explain, in step-by-step detail, how the job is going to be accomplished. The very act of voicing the process aloud to another person helps solidify the procedure in your own mind—even though you are, of course, thoroughly prepared.

Summary

1. Painting is a lonely business; having another person involved can help with creative input as well as physical labor.
2. A perfect partnership is formed when all parties share the same business ethics, have complementary painting styles and the personalities mesh.
3. Not all partnerships need be created equal; a partnership based on a disproportionate distribution of work and profit can work well, provided all parties accept their roles and responsibilities right off the bat. Preparing a partnership agreement will alleviate any confusion about the status and expectations of the partnership.
4. Determine if you want to hire an assistant as an employee or as an independent contractor. Be sure to iron out a hiring agreement before bringing in someone to help you on the job.
5. A hard-working assistant is a treasure and should be paid accordingly.

Chapter 11

Working With Interior Designers and Other Professionals

Establishing a good working relationship with one or two interior designers can really help launch a decorative painting business. Some designers are easier to work with than others, as in all working relationships. Notice I use the term *work with* rather than *work for*. A good working relationship comes when both parties respect and appreciate the talents and efforts of the other. It is wonderful when you have a relationship with an interior designer who has a good understanding of your abilities as a decorative artist.

Be sure to keep your work at the forefront of the designer's attention, and always be sure the designer stays up to date with what is happening in your business. For example, it will be very restrictive if you have a designer who thinks of you as a stenciler, when in fact you added wall glazing and faux finishing to your business the previous year. It is up to you to keep designers informed of the changes that occur in your business and of your growth as an artist. Mailing photo postcards or artistic and colorful card-stock postcards is a good way to keep your work in the forefront of the designer's mind.

Not all interior designers are a joy to work with—I've worked for designers who are very controlling and want to supervise the placement of every leaf on a vine, and others who are so inexperienced they look to me for design suggestions. Luckily, most designers fall somewhere in between those extremes. You will have to decide for yourself if you want to pursue working with a difficult interior designer. Sometimes the exposure and the type of work they will bring to you warrant tolerating their personality quirks, but there will be other designers who simply are not worth the headache. Be careful about burning your bridges with any interior designers, however, because, as in all professions, these people often network with each other, and you do not want to get a reputation for being unprofessional.

The designers with whom I have the most difficult working relationships are the designers who I say work in the ''hurry up and wait'' mode. They will call me in a panic, requesting an immediate meeting with the client, rushed samples and estimates, only to find out the job won't be scheduled for months. I have learned that it is best to accommodate these designers as much as possible, but not at the expense of my other clients and my responsibilities.

When you are new to the industry, try not to let interior designers intimidate you, as some may try to do. Be confident in your abilities, definitive and professional in your business dealings, and you will be well on the road to establishing a good rapport.

Making Contacts

Focusing your marketing tactics on decorators and interior designers is a great place to start. Even established decorative painters should continue to market themselves to local designers. Designers like to feel they are finding something new—and who knows better what is new in the decorative painting fields than you? The basic marketing strategies outlined previously still hold true, but with a different slant. As most designers are ''visual'' people, you will need to grab their attention with lively, colorful photographs.

Connecting with established designers with a large clientele is a worthy goal. Do some investigative work. Which designers names keep popping up over and over? These are the ones you will want to target your marketing toward. But often, these decorators are the hardest to convince to hire you. Perservere.

The best way to get your foot in the door is to send a letter of introduction, along with your business card, asking to arrange a meeting. Follow up the letter with a phone call to schedule an appointment, at the designer's convenience, to present your portfolio and sample boards. Sometimes the designer will give you a call, but that is rare, so be sure to make follow-up phone calls yourself. By doing this, you have a better feel for what your prospects of working with that particular designer will be. If she tells you that they already have someone, do not be deterred. Simply state that everyone has a different painting style, and you would like to show her yours. If the designer cuts you off by saying she is not interested, ask why not. Knowing her reasons will make the rejection a little less personal or, if you find her reasons invalid, perhaps you could still manage to get your foot in the door by gently explaining why it would be worth her while to see you.

I do not recommend making cold calls or stopping in without an appointment. Not only is this rude, but you could catch the designer at a busy time or in a bad mood. Sending a letter first allows time for your name to register, and the designer will be more likely to meet with you.

Showcase Houses

Showcase houses are community-sponsored charity events where local interior designers pool their talents and transform a house into a decorating

I prepared a one-page color-copied flier with photos of work I had just completed and sent it with a cover letter, my promotional letter, to all the designers listed in the yellow pages.

feast. Tours and charity events are held throughout the time the house is open to the public.

Volunteering your services to designers or the committee in charge of the event is a great way to network with designers. You will meet dozens under one roof. You will see whose work you admire as well as whose work leaves you cold. You have a chance to figure out whose personality and style will click best with yours.

It is rare to be paid for your time when working on a showcase home, but there is usually enough of a budget to cover the cost of materials. Clarifying payment before painting will avoid any unpleasant surprises. It never hurts to ask if the budget will allow payment for your time, as well as your materials, because each showcase home has a different budget.

Be sure that your business name will be included in the brochure and that your cards will be handed out while the house is open. I have worked for designers who have refused to leave my cards, instead wanting the public to hire me through the designer, thus ensuring they will get a cut. I have a hard time swallowing this. Past history has shown me that the paper trail is too hard for the average person to follow, and I end up not getting the referral at all. Moral of the story: Be sure to have an agreement with the designers up front to include your name in their promotional materials.

I try to work in one showcase home each year. This has become harder as my schedule has become fuller, but it is still good advertising and good exposure for my business. Also, in my area, the general public is impressed with you when you are associated with a showcase home. This type of credibility always enhances my business's esteem. Every year I meet new designers and, best of all, because decorative painting is such a hot topic, often my work is photographed for newspapers and magazines, giving me even more exposure.

Working in a showcase home also allows the designers and the public to see what feats you are capable of performing. While you are working in the house, be sure to have plenty of your business cards on hand—or in your apron pocket while working—to give out to the curious passerby.

Billing Arrangements

Each designer has a different billing arrangement or payment method she prefers. This is something that should be cleared up at the first meeting (without a client present). Some designers prefer to bill the client themselves, so you will bill the designer. Others prefer for you to bill the client directly, adding a referral percentage for the designer to your bill. And some others will step out of the billing equation entirely and allow you to bill the client directly, with no referral fee attached.

When you will be billing the designer directly, it will be the designer who signs the contracts, pays your deposit and is responsible for timely final payment. Be clear with the designer that you expect to be paid upon completion of the work—not when the designer is paid by the client. The designer's billing practices may not match yours.

If you are billing the client directly with a referral fee included, be sure to make an extra copy of the invoice to forward to the designer along with the check for her referral fee. And if you are lucky enough to have a designer that steps out of the billing process altogether, be sure to at least send her a thank-you note for the referral. If it's a big job, you might consider sending her a thank-you gift.

Never discuss your pricing, fees or payment method with the decorator's client unless you have authorization from the designer to do so. When you are billing the designer, it is common for her to add a percentage for her time and efforts to the final bill. Some clients are very naïve about standard billing practices of interior designers, and it is in your best interests not to educate them. Not only will you be caught in the middle, but the designer will think it very unprofessional of you to be discussing pricing with *her* client.

Subcontracting

Subcontracting, loosely translated, means that your business will complete all, or part, of another business's work contract. You will want to present yourself as a subcontractor, not as an employee. This means that you will be responsible for paying your own taxes out of what you are paid, but will be blanketed by the contractor's insurance policies. This is how I present myself to all the designers and contractors for whom I work.

As a subcontractor, you will be expected have your own fully established business, complete with liability insurance. The interior designer, or any other business hiring you, will expect you to pay your own taxes, not withholding taxes as they would for their employees. At the end of the year, instead of furnishing you with a W-2, they will send you a Form 1099. This form alerts the IRS that you have been paid but they have not, and *all* income needs to be reported on your tax returns. The benefit for being a subcontractor is that you will be covered by the hiring company for Workman's Compensation insurance. Although technically you would also be covered under their liability insurance, most companies will require proof of insurance showing that you, too, are covered by liability insurance.

Referral Fees

A referral fee is a percentage tacked onto your bill as payment for the client referral by the designer. Referral fees vary among designers. The norm is 10 to 20 percent. Referral fees are only paid when the client is billed directly by the decorative painter and not by the designer. When you are billing the designer and not the client, you will not pay the designer a referral fee because it is assumed the designer will be adding a percentage to your bill.

Pay the agreed-upon referral fee on time. Include a copy of the billing invoice and a thank-you note to the designer along with your check. This helps build goodwill and strengthens your working relationship with the designer.

Ethics

One of the biggest mistakes decorative painters make is to question a decision made by the designer, especially in front of the client. If you believe what the designer wants you to do cannot be accomplished under any circumstances, or if there is an easier way, thus saving time and money, you can discuss this with the designer privately—never in front of the client.

Never discuss decorating choices with the client. Sometimes the client is uncomfortable with a decision the designer has made and is looking to you for confirmation. You can gently suggest the client talk to the designer, reminding him that he has to live with the designer's decisions, and he should be happy with the final results. If you get the chance, tell the designer the client's concerns. Never get in the middle of a problem between the decorator and the client.

Should the client decide to contact you personally for more work, without going through the designer, be sure to call the designer and inform her that you have undertaken another commission with her client. Never try to cut the designer out of the billing equation, even to save a referral fee, unless you have gotten permission from the designer to do so. Remember, that client found you because of the designer.

Which brings us to exclusivity rights. Every so often you will come across a designer who insists that you work solely for her and no one else. This working relationship is bondage at best. Never accept such an agreement, even if the designer promises to keep you extremely busy. There are no guarantees that she will, or even can, keep you working enough to turn down other work.

Working With Contractors, Architects and Other Professionals

Making contact with builders, painting contractors and architects is another great way to increase your workload and widen your market. While working with interior designers is mostly likely to be the best way to get your foot into a client's door, these other professionals have good, but different, access to clients who need your decorative painting.

Targeting your marketing to building contractors will also gain you access to new clients. Contact builders whose work you admire and who have a good business reputation, especially those who are working in new construction and housing developments, as these markets are ripe for decorating. Painting in model homes can bring as much exposure to your business as painting a showcase home. Be sure that the builder will keep your business cards on display and will refer you to prospective customers.

If your decorative painting business is geared toward working on walls, develop a good business relationship with a reliable painting contractor. This will be more of a two-way street than your other professional contacts. You will need someone to whom you can refer the prep-work phase of your jobs. You can offer to refer the painting contractor to your clientele in exchange for his referrals of your work to his customers.

I have a good relationship with a painting contractor who uses me as her subcontractor for all her faux finish work. She has a good reputation in the community, which is important: I would not want my name associated with an unreliable painter. On the other side of the coin, she knows that I am not a flaky artist and that I, too, am a reliable businesswoman. It's good for her business to be able to offer the classy touch of decorative painting to her customers, and it's good for my business to know I have

"The very first job I ever did (23 years ago) was two murals in a children's room for the largest home show in the country. I was fresh out of college and felt lucky to land such a job. One of the murals was a woodland scene in the little girl's room, and the designer wanted me to paint the inside of my trees yellow. I thought, 'yellow?' I balked, and never did paint the tree yellow. He never used me again. He went on to be the biggest name designer in town. I learned that I am a service business and I am being paid to do what someone wants, no matter if I like it or not."

—GARY LORD

North Shore Wall Design

D E C O R A T I V E   P A I N T I N G

1023 Oakwood Avenue — Wilmette, Illinois 60091
Phone (847) 853-0904

Statement

Castino Painting   April 10, 1997
1504 Happ Road
Northbrook, IL 60062

Client: Henry (128 Gateway, Wilmette, IL 60091)
   Oil glaze (BM #1095), parchment finish on living room walls.

Labor: 6 hrs. @ $40/hr.	$240.00
Labor: 6 hrs. @ $20/hr.	$120.00
Materials:	$48.00
BALANCE DUE:	$408.00

Thank You!

An invoice of billing statement for subcontracting work

reliable painting help when I need it. I have provided sample boards to the painting contractor to show her clients to help her sell my services.

Architects, like designers, are always looking for new and innovative design concepts, and can make for an exciting working relationship. Again, target respected and well-known architectural firms who have a solid client base. You will want to provide these firms with samples and photos of your work to present to their clientele.

When working with these professionals, you will need to follow the same code of ethics as you would with interior designers. Establish, at your initial meeting, how to best handle billing, referral fees and scheduling. Again, each one will probably have his own method of operation within which he will want you to function. When in doubt, it's always better to ask what the expectations are than to just operate on blind faith.

Summary

1. Target your marketing to interior designers in your area by sending letters of introduction, followed up with a phone call requesting a meeting to show them your portfolio.
2. Establishing a "work with" rather than a "work for" relationship with interior designers works best for everyone.
3. Expose your work to the public through a showcase house. It is a fine way to meet lots of decorators under one roof.
4. Clarify with the interior designer what her preferred billing method will be, as every designer will have a different billing method and expect a different referral fee.
5. Establish yourself as a subcontractor when working for other businesses.
6. Don't meddle with the relationship between client and designer.
7. Contact building contractors, architects and other professionals as another good means to market your business.

Chapter 12

Craftsmanship

A craftsman can be defined as an artisan who performs his trade or her handicraft with polished skill and dexterity. Personal integrity is a key ingredient, as is devoting the necessary time and practice to perfecting your technique and artistry. Combining honor with skill will make you a master craftsman—and this is a worthy goal for all of us.

Becoming a Master Craftsman

The following sections describe some of the steps you can take along this path.

1. Perfect Your Craft.

The first step to becoming a master craftsman is to master the skills and develop the talent to perform your craft at the highest level of dexterity. While experience will be your best teacher, try to study, practice and learn something new about your craft every day. Learn from others. Keep searching for new and better ways to achieve the end result of your craft. Any time you can achieve something quicker or easier, while still maintaining the quality, you have taken a big step toward becoming a master craftsman.

It might be interesting to note that no one ever "arrives" or "gets there," because even the most experienced craftsman must keep learning and evolving as an artist. Learning is essential to growth. Without growth, all creativity and artistry dies a slow and ugly death. However, while this ongoing process continues, you should kick your business ethics and personal integrity into high gear.

2. Satisfy the Customer.

Although several clichés come to mind about satisfying the customer, this philosophy is the cornerstone of all successful businesses. Try your hardest to please all concerned, even if this means making a sacrifice. The benefits of a satisfied customer will far outweigh any inconvenience on your part. Of course, we've all encountered the one customer who will not be satisfied, no matter how many hoops you jump through trying to please him. In these circumstances, when you know in your heart that you have done your best and tried your hardest, it's best to terminate the working relationship. How you handle this will be up to you and the provisions of your contract.

Complete each job down to the very last detail as promised or, better yet, give a little extra. This builds goodwill with your clientele, and that type of goodwill comes back to you tenfold.

3. Be Professional.

Presentation is everything, and how you present yourself is a testimony to your personal integrity and style. Being professional is not synonymous with being cold, aloof and distant to your clients—being professional means having your act together. You can be charming and charismatic and still be professional. Be organized—or at least maintain the illusion that you are organized by being prepared. Having your business paperwork polished and shipshape adds much to your professional presentation.

"What's the worst that can happen? I can always paint over it."

—NIKI GAMBOA

Being an artist gives us limitless choices when it comes to dressing for success. Dressing for business appointments will require a different style than dressing to paint. Obviously you will not want to paint in your Sunday best, but I think the time often comes to retire a beloved painting garment. Avoid giving the illusion that you cannot control where the paint winds up! In any case, be true to your own sense of style, and you cannot go wrong.

4. Do Your Best.

Never cut corners. It always shows, and if not to your customer, it will to you. Trying to slip something by will damage your personal *and* business integrity. Even if the customer doesn't notice the haphazard application, you will know, and it will eat away at you and your sense of self.

5. Pay Attention to Details.

If you want your business to thrive, you must pay attention to the details. Be picky, picky, picky! And accept nothing but the best from the people who work for or with you. Systematically check and recheck to be sure that you complete the job down to the last detail as promised, that everything is clean and tidy and that you are satisfied that you have done your best.

6. Keep Your Word.

Honor and be faithful to your word. Live up to your promises to your clients and to yourself. If you say you are going to do something, by all means *do it*, and do it within the promised time frame. Do not miss or "forget" appointments if at all possible. If for any reason you cannot keep your word, the best plan is to be honest and tell it like it is. The goodwill of your business depends on it.

7. Be Honest.

Honesty still is, and always will be, the best policy. But there have been consultations where I have said, "sure I can do that" and left, wondering "just how in the heck *am* I going to do that?" Listen to your gut instincts; they will not let you down. If the prospects are a reach, but reasonable, I feel this is a harmless stretch of the truth. Of course, if the client asks, "Have you ever done anything like this before?" it is best to answer truthfully, "No, but

I *do* feel confident that I can do this.'' However, you will be doing yourself and your client a huge disservice if you truly are not qualified for the project and get in over your head. Again, your instincts will be screaming at you: You had better walk away from this job!

We all know people who pretend they know the answers to every question, even when they haven't a clue what they are talking about. This can be particularly damaging when there is paint involved. If you do not know, it is much better to admit ignorance, and offer to research an answer to the question, than to blunder and bluff your way through.

8. Be Flexible.

Everyone changes their mind from time to time. Accept this with grace, but be upfront about any price differences that may result from these changes. Minor changes need not necessarily result in an added charge if you view the change as adding that little extra touch to satisfy the client. However, major overhauls that affect the total design are another story. Again, be tactful and diplomatic, but be firm about what those changes mean to you and to the client. Do not assume that the client automatically understands that the changes will mean a different price estimate. Tell them!

9. Put Your Own Taste Aside.

We artists are an opinionated lot, but we need to put aside our own personal taste. In the end, the cliché ''the customer is always right'' must be honored, even if you hate what you are doing. Remember, it's not you who has to live with the end result. Tell the client what you love about it, even when you are cringing inside. ''Yes, the walls match the pea green color of your sofa perfectly.'' There is always something positive to be said, and if not, follow Mom's advice: ''If you can't say anything nice, say nothing at all.'' If we all had the same taste, the world would be very bland indeed.

10. Do Your Homework.

Like the Boy Scout motto, ''Be Prepared!'' By doing your homework, you will be able to begin work with confidence. This could mean anything from learning a new technique *before* you begin the job, making proofs to test your stencils and colors, having all the supplies and equipment you need to complete the job or researching for design concepts. Just like in school, you may think you can bluff your way around being unprepared, but it always shows through. And if it doesn't, being unprepared will fluster you and erode your self-esteem.

11. Never Leave the Customer Unhappy.

Even if you have completed the job to the letter of your agreement, if the customer isn't happy, the job is not complete. A decorative painting business thrives on word-of-mouth referrals, and a happy client is the essential ingredient. Sometimes you have to swallow your pride, your annoyance and your ego to satisfy your customer. Do it with a smile on your face.

Ten Commandments for the Decorative Painter

1. Make Quality, Craftsmanship and Personal Integrity Top Priority for Your Business.

Always do your best work, and do not cut corners. Pay attention to details. Autograph your work with pride.

2. Be Professional.

Be businesslike in your dress, appearance and presentation. Have an impressive portfolio that will sell your work for you. Order printed business cards and printed stationery for your estimates, contracts and billings.

3. Keep Your Word.

Be on time for all appointments, and make a phone call as soon as possible if you are delayed. Return phone calls promptly. Present completed samples when promised. Start the job when scheduled, or reschedule as early as possible should a conflict arise.

4. Do Your Homework.

Know your craft and be prepared for the job. Discuss everything you are going to do with the client, but also put it in writing. Show up the day of the job ready to work.

5. Be Flexible.

Everyone changes their mind from time to time. Accept changes with grace and be up front about the price changes involved in making changes. Offer your client your professional opinion, but remember that the final decision rests with the client, so do not force your opinion on your client.

6. Be Honest.

Better to admit that you don't know the answer to a question than to bluff your way through. While I do believe in stretching your abilities, sometimes it's better to walk away from a job you are truly not qualified for than to get in over your head.

7. Be Neat and Courteous.

Leave the job site as clean or cleaner than you found it. Protect and cover every surface. Careful taping saves time in cleanup and helps protect the client's property. Do not make your client's home your own. Bring your own food and drink, and use your own telephone. Do not leave your trash for the client to dispose of.

8. Don't Be Afraid to Stretch/Push Yourself.

There is a fine line between knowing your limits and pushing yourself. Listen to your instincts. The best way to conquer new heights is to stretch beyond what you comfortably know you can accomplish effortlessly. Keep learning new skills—no one knows it all.

9. Be Kind to Yourself.

The work is physically and mentally demanding. Reward yourself often. Take time off to recharge your creative batteries whenever possible. Soak in hot Epsom salts or luxurious bubble baths. Do stretching and relaxation exercises to keep overworked muscles happy.

10. *Never* Leave a Client Unhappy.

The best advertising you will ever have is a satisfied customer. Be sure that clients are happy with the job, and they, in turn, will tell their friends and family about you.

Chapter 13

Caring for Your Most Important Asset—You!

To put it plainly, you are the most important and valuable asset of your business: Without you there is no business. All the education, instruction and training you undertake increases the substance of this considerable asset. The savvy combination of common sense, book learning, tenacity, chutzpah, perseverance and heart makes the "right stuff." You must nurture and protect this exceptional asset!

This business can be physically demanding and mentally challenging. Learning to accommodate several clients and commissions at once is exciting, but it also can be daunting and can quickly become overwhelming. Balancing the creative mind with the business mind often feels like a juggling act with one too many plates in the air. Everyone handles stress differently—some thrive on chaos, and others panic when life gets hectic. The following techniques to control muscle and mental fatigue, while at the same time warding off exhaustion and burnout, are important to keeping your best business asset in top shape!

Controlling Muscle Fatigue

Whether you are painting in big, bold, sweeping strokes or a small, detailed fine line, you will soon discover muscles groups that you did not know previously existed inside your body. There is almost no painting technique that doesn't involve an isometric hold (opposing muscles contracted into a locked position) or repetitive motion (repeating the same movement over and over). Both of these motions will eventually strain and injure muscles. The only way to avoid muscle strain is to allow the damaged muscle time to heal. Ice the muscle, allow time for rest and take anti-inflammatory medications. Then you must strengthen the muscles with weight-training exercises. Strengthening the upper body muscles will help you avoid chronic pain and long-term injury.

Stretching before and after you begin to paint is an excellent way to keep the muscles from screaming back at you later. If you are doing a particularly painful application, like ceilings or floors, you will need to take breaks often to stretch the muscles to relieve the tension. When you are finished for the day, treat yourself to a long soak in a hot tub with Epsom salts or a relaxing aromatherapy bath product, which helps relax and soothe your tired muscles. However, if the pain is chronic, you will need to ice down the muscle, rest it and allow it time to heal. Should the pain continue, you should see your doctor.

Regular exercise and healthy eating habits will go a long way to increase your stamina and job productivity. Exercise and healthy eating habits will also play a huge role in your mental health. Try to drink at least three liters (3.2qt) of water every day. Your body's signals for thirst can often be confused with fatigue symptoms.

And finally, indulge in a therapeutic massage as often as your budget will allow. The masseuse can help you learn which muscles you are overworking and need to pay special attention to by relaxing them when tensed. This wonderful treat will leave you purring like a kitten.

"Our business is such a personal expression of our being, most of us carry some form of insecurity throughout our careers. We all have to deal with this in our own way, and I choose to do it with as much humor as I can muster."

—NORA MUELLER

Conquering Mental Fatigue

Getting the right brain (your artistic nature) to work in harmony with your left brain (your business nature) is quite a challenge. I have this mental picture of my brain as a lion tamer. My left brain is cracking the whip, forcing my right brain to perform artistically as it roars loudly, but complies nonetheless. Needless to say, this tug-of-war between cranial regions can produce mental fatigue. And prolonged mental fatigue is the preface to burnout, which must be avoided at all costs. There are a few things you can do to relieve the pressure on your gray cells, and taking these precautions will quickly extinguish the flames of burnout before you are charred beyond recognition. When you start to feel a little crispy, remember:

1. *Keep your sense of humor.* Laughter, seeing the humorous side, will always relieve your mental strain and brighten your outlook on life.

2. *Make to-do lists.* When your head becomes filled with the minutiae of all the billions of details you need to remember, take time to write it all down. Make a list of everything that is bothering you. The physical act of writing lets your left brain stop nagging you long enough to allow your right brain to get down to the business of creating.

3. *Take a nature break* and spend some time out of doors, no matter what the weather is like. Just a few minutes to breathe fresh air, feel the sun on your skin, study the sky and cloud formations, watch a bird fly past, make a snowball, pick a flower or go barefoot in the grass will renew your energy level and refresh your spirit.

4. *Exercise daily.* Even a short walk will help get oxygen to your brain, and the brain chemicals (endorphins) released during aerobic exercise help the brain to function better.

5. *Eat regularly.* A brief interlude to have snacks and perhaps some chocolate will give your painting a fresh new perspective.

6. *Paint something for the sheer joy of painting,* not only for work. This

helps remind you of the reason you fell in love with the craft in the first place.

7. *Stay organized.* Take the time to straighten out your paperwork and painting supplies before it becomes such a large mess that it becomes impossible to untangle. Messes are very stressful, and will quickly scatter your energy and drain your ability to focus.

8. *Seek assistance,* gather support and rally the troops during the busy spells. Delegate as much responsibility as possible, and pass on every task that you do not *have* to do yourself.

9. *Take an artist's holiday.* This is a variation on the theme of the proverbial mental health day. An artist's holiday is a day set aside to spark your imagination. Go to a museum, go to the theater or go shopping in ethnic neighborhoods or stores. Even if you don't sew, go to the largest textile store you can find. Rediscover nature by taking a hike through the woods or the local botanical gardens. Go anywhere that ignites your soul with color, passion and life. A word of caution: Do not take your children, or anyone who will be a wet blanket, on your artist's holiday. It's okay to be a bit selfish and nurture your own flight of fancy.

10. *Reward yourself.* Pat yourself on the back often, and indulge yourself with a little treat when you've accomplished a big project.

Dousing the Flames of Burnout

If the quick fixes mentioned above don't seem to douse the flames of burnout, you probably have a more serious case. True burnout is the hopeless feeling you get when you have too much to do, with too many responsibilities and not enough time get everything completed in the manner you want. If you function this way for too long, you will begin to feel like blackened toast. As you first begin your decorative painting business, the notion of burnout will seem laughable. But many established artists have crashed and burned because they did not recognize, nor know how to manage, the symptoms of burnout. Beware of the symptoms: the fleeting desire to go get a "real" job; being totally exhausted even after a full night's sleep; suffering from recurring or chronic illness; or finding yourself short-tempered and overly cranky. There are other dreaded symptoms of burnout, which I call the four P danger signals: Procrastination, Pessimism and Peevish Perfectionism. If you can use any of these four words to describe your current frame of mind, it is time to perform triage and salve the blisters.

What to Do If You Are Well Done and Fully Cooked

1. Recognizing the symptoms of burnout is half the battle. Usually you are so entrenched in the daily barrage that you only notice how awful you feel when a respite comes. A couple days of rest, relaxation and a little fun will be just the ticket.

2. Take stock of all you have accomplished and give yourself a good pat on the back. It's easy to beat yourself up over the things that you aren't getting done, but don't fail to recognize all the many, many wondrous tasks you have performed so well.

3. Stop procrastinating. Whatever it is, do it now. Ask yourself, "If not now, when will I find the time?" The answer is usually laughable, so just do it now so you can rest easier. Avoiding work is much more time-consuming and harder than just doing the task in the first place.

4. Do not allow those little pessimistic voices to sing inside your head. You know the ones I mean. Those voices that say, "You can't do anything right" or "You should have done that better." When that

"Persevere! When you are first starting out it's a good idea to have another source of income. Don't expect to make it overnight. But I've never been happier in my life."

—MARGE LOWERY

a capella choir kicks in and starts singing those nasty tunes, you need to shut it off, shut it up or turn off the volume. The voice of self-doubt and fear will erode your sense of self, and that voice must be silenced.

5. Rein in your perfectionist tendencies. We all strive to be the best we can be, but trying to achieve perfection will, over time, kill your creative spirit and fan the flames of burnout. Giving yourself permission to say ''good enough'' instead of ''it's perfect'' is the greatest gift you will ever receive.

6. And if all else fails, force yourself to take a vacation where you can play, be pampered and fed well, and have some fun with your loved ones. Get reacquainted with life away from paint and a brush.

And Finally...

I have heard numerous times, "Do what you love, and the money will follow." This wonderful sentiment has certainly held true for me and my life. I still believe there are other professions I could have chosen that would have netted me a higher income, but there could not possibly be a profession that I love more. And with that said, I find that all I *have* is all that I *need*.

It's very exciting to be able to take a design concept from somewhere in the far corners of my mind, be able to express it with enough enthusiasm to excite my client, problem-solve until I can figure the best methods to accomplish the task and see the work unfold into something even greater than we all imagined. It's a heady experience. That's when I realize there is a higher power at work that is greater than just little ol' me. I credit my success to making that spiritual connection. You see, I believe that the powers of this universe love artists because artists appreciate and create beauty. That's our job. When we honor that job, we connect into a resource that is unexplainably powerful.

So as you begin to follow this path, accept that gifts are going to come to you in ways that will surprise you, from places you did not know even existed—just as you need them most. You cannot create art, music, drama or literature unless you are connected spiritually. You will not be successful unless you recognize and give thanks for the gift you've been given. Do not question that power, simply accept it, be grateful for it and remember to acknowledge it.

When I have the most problems with my work, it is because I am blocking that natural energy flow, or egotistically trying to go it alone. When I relax enough to accept divine intervention and listen with my whole being, it all comes into order. It requires discipline to take the time to stop the world long enough to listen truly to the powers within. If you choose not to listen, the universe will take its divine plan elsewhere and find another willing host for creating beauty in the world. Julia Cameron, in her book *The Artist's Way*, called these voices ''Marching Orders.'' They are different voices from the self-doubt and ego (which do hold raging fights within my psyche). They are much clearer voices. My marching orders insisted that I write this book.

If you are reading this book, you too have probably been given marching orders. Do not be afraid to take that first step, even if it seems like a giant leap to you right now. Make the commitment with enthusiasm, enjoy the process and celebrate your successes, no matter how small.

Recommended Reading

Theory and Technique

Binney-Smith. *The Handbook of Decorative Art Techniques.* Binney-Smith, Inc., 1992.

Blake, Wendon. *Getting Started in Drawing.* North Light Books, 1991.

Brookes, Mona. *Drawing with Children.* J.P. Tarcher, Inc., 1986.

Chijiiwa, Hideake. *Color Harmony: A Guide to Creative Color Combinations.* Rockport Publishers (North Light Books), 1987.

Dalley, Terrance. *Complete Guide to Illustration and Design.* Chartwell Books, 1981.

Decker, Peggy. *Design Press Your Home.* Back Street, Inc., 1996.

Edwards, Betty. *Drawing on the Right Side of the Brain.* J.P. Tarcher, Inc., 1979.

Griffel, Lois. *Painting the Impressionist Landscape: Lessons in Interpreting Light and Color.* Watson/Guptill Publications, 1994.

Harris, Hazel. *Painting Solutions: Buildings.* Wellfleet Press, 1991.

Hebblewhite, Ian. *The North Light Handbook of Artist's Materials.* North Light Books, 1985.

Martin, Judy. *Airbrush Painting Techniques.* North Light Books, 1994.

Martin, Judy. *Color: How to See It/How to Paint It.* Book Sales, 1994.

Metzger, Phil. *Perspective Without Pain.* North Light Books, 1992.

Norling, Ernest. *Perspective Drawing.* Walter Foster Publishing, 1989.

Shaw, Jackie. *Tole Technique & Decorative Arts.* Deco Design Studio, 1974.

Smith, Ray. *How to Draw & Paint What You See.* Alfred Knopf, 1981.

Tate, Elizabeth. *The North Light Illustrated Book of Painted Techniques.* North Light Books, 1986.

Watson, Barb. *The ABC's of Color.* P.O. Box 1467, Moreno Valley, CA 92556.

Stenciling Books

Barnett, Helen, and Suzy Smith. *Stencilling*. Salem House, 1987.

Bishop, Adele, and Cele Lord. *The Art of Decorative Stenciling*. Penguin Books, 1976.

Britton, Susan, and Jackie Looney. *Floral Patterns for Stenciling*. Sterling Publishing Co., 1986.

Day, JoAnne. *The Complete Book of Stencilcraft*. Dover Publications, 1987.

Fraser, Bridget. *Stencilling: A Design & Source Book*. Henry Holt & Co., 1987.

Gauss, Jane. *The Complete Book of Wall Stenciling*. Plaid Enterprises, 1984.

Gauss, Jane. *Stenciling Techniques: A Complete Guide to Traditional and Contemporary Designs for the Home*. Watson/Guptill, 1995.

LeGrice, Lyn. *The Art of Stenciling*. Clarkson Potter, 1986.

LeGrice, Lyn. *The Stencilled House*. Simon & Schuster, 1988.

MacCarthy, Mary. *Decorative Stencils for Your Home*. North Light Books, 1996.

Richie, Kathy Fillion. *Stencilling*. Henry Holt & Co., 1995.

Roche, Tony, and Patricia Monahan. *Decorating with Stencils*. Abbyville Press, 1995.

Stott, Rowena, and Jane Cheshire. *The Country Diary Book of Stenciling*. Viking, 1988.

Visser, Jill, and Michael Flinn. *Stenciling*. Harmony Books, 1988.

Waring, Janet. *Early American Stencils on Walls & Furniture*. Dover Publications, 1968.

Warrender, Carolyn. *Carolyn Warrender's Book of Stenciling*. Harmony Books, 1988.

Murals and Trompe L'Oeil

Cass, Caroline. *Modern Murals: Grand Illusions in Interior Decoration*. Whitney Library of Design, 1988.

Chambers, Karen S. *Trompe L'Oeil at Home*. Rizzoli, 1991.

McCloud, Kevin. *Decorative Style*. Simon & Schuster, 1990.

Milman, Miriam. *Trompe L'Oeil Architecture*. Rizzoli, 1986.

Milman, Miriam. *Trompe L'Oeil Painting*. Rizzoli, 1983.

Monahan, Patricia. *Landscape Painting*. North Light Books, 1985.

Plant, Tim. *Painted Illusions*. Ward Lock, Ltd., 1991.

Powell, William F. *Clouds & Skyscapes*. Walter Foster Publishing, 1989.

Rust, Graham. *The Painted House*. Alfred Knopf, 1988.

Seligman, Patricia. *How to Paint Trees, Flowers & Foliage*. North Light Books, 1994.

Seligman, Patricia. *Painting Murals: Images, Ideas and Techniques*. North Light Books, 1988.

Faux Finishing Books

Bennell, Jennifer. *Master Works.* North Light Books, 1994.

Bradshaw, Ray. *1,200 Paint Effects for the Home Decorator.* North Light Books, 1997.

Cavelle, Simon. *The Encyclopedia of Decorative Paint Techniques.* Running Press, 1994.

Drucker, Mindy, and Pierre Finkelstein. *Recipes for Surfaces.* Simon & Schuster, 1990.

Drucker, Mindy, and Nancy Rosen. *Recipes for Surfaces II.* Simon & Schuster, 1995.

Hemming, Charles. *Paint Finishes.* Chartwell Books, 1985.

Home Decorating Institute. *Decorative Painting/Arts & Crafts for the Home.* Cy Decoss, Inc., 1994.

Innes, Jocasta. *Decorating With Paint.* Harmony Books, 1986.

Innes, Jocosta. *Paint Magic.* Pantheon Books, 1982.

Marx, Ina Brousseau. *Professional Painted Finishes.* Watson/Guptill, 1991.

McCloud, Kevin. *Kevin McCloud's Complete Book of Paint and Decorative Techniques.* Simon & Schuster, 1996.

Meschbach, Karl-Heinz. *Mastering Faux Fundamentals.* Meschbach & Friends, 1996.

Meyer, Phillip. *Creative Paint Finishes for the Home.* North Light Books, 1995.

Miller, Judith, and Michael Miller. *Period Finishes & Effects.* Rizzoli, 1991.

Ridley, Jessica. *Finishing Touches.* Charles Scribner & Sons, 1988.

Sloan, Annie, and Kate Gwynn. *Decorative Paint Techniques.* Crescent Books, 1989.

Spencer, Stuart. *Marbling.* Harmon Books, 1989.

Wagstaff, Liz. *Paint Recipes.* Chronicle Books, 1995.

Wassong, Lisa. *Fantastic Painted Finishes.* Chronicle Books, 1994.

Wilson, Althea. *Paint Works: The Art of Decorative Paint.* Fawcett/Columbine, 1988.

Painted Furniture and Decoration

Cooper, Kathy, and Jan Hershey. *The Complete Book of Floorcloths.* Lark Books, 1997.

Fisher, Rosie. *Painting Furniture: A Practical Guide.* Little, Brown & Co., 1988.

Gray, Susan. *Decorative Painting of the World.* Thunder Bay Press, 1995.

Guegan, Yannick, and Roger LePuil. *Handbook of Painted Decoration.* W.W. Norton & Co., 1996.

McGraw, Sheila. *Painting and Decorating Furniture.* Firefly Books, 1997.

Midkiff, Pat. *The Complete Book of Stenciling: Furniture Decoration and Restoration.* Sterling Publishing, 1978.

O'Neil, Isabel. *The Art of the Painted Finish for Furniture & Decoration.* William Morrow, 1971.

Rees, Yvonne. *Decorative Painting.* Chartwell Books, 1988.

Thompson, Julia Hamilton. *Creative Ideas for Decorating,* Oxmoor House, 1987.

Winfield, Barbara. *The Complete Book of Home Details.* Crescent Books, 1993.

Business

Barnett, E. Thorpe. *Write Your Own Business Contracts.* Oasis Press, 1997.

Brabec, Barbara. *Handmade for Profit.* M. Evans & Co., 1996.

Caputo, Kathryn. *How to Start Making Money With Your Crafts.* Betterway Books, 1995.

DeWalt, Suzanne. *How to Start a Home-Based Inerior Design Business.* The Globe, Pequot Press, 1997.

Halverson, Kate. *Systems for Success: A How-To Manual for Today's Interior Designer.* Weston Communications, 1990.

Knackstedt, Mary, and Laura Haney. *The Interior Design Business Handbook.* Whitney Library of Design, 1988.

Pinson, Linda, and Jerry Jinnett. *Steps to Small Business Start-Up.* Dearborn Trade, 1996.

Siegel, Harry, and Alan Siegel. *A Guide to Business Principles and Practices for Interior Designers.* Whitney Library of Design, 1982.

Victoroff, Gregory. *The Visual Artist's Business & Legal Guide.* Prentice Hall Trade, 1995.

Miscellaneous

Bayles, David, and Ted Orland. *Art & Fear: Observations on the Periods and Rewards of Artmaking.* Capra Press, 1994.

Cameron, Julia. *The Artist's Way: A Spiritual Path to Higher Creativity.* Tarcher/Putnam, 1992.

Cameron, Julia. *The Vein of Gold: A Journey to Your Creative Heart.* Tarcher/Putnam, 1996.

Von Oech, Roger. *A Whack on the Side of the Head: How To Be More Creative.* Warner Books, 1990.

Sources for Catalogs of Books

Dover Publications
31 East Second Street
Mineola, NY 11501
Request: Dover Pictorial Archive, Dover Clip Art Sampler, Dover Crafts & Hobbies Catalog, Dover Catalog of Full Color Design Books

JoSonja's Folk Art Studio
P.O. Box 9080
Eureka, CA 95501
(707) 445-9306
Request: Color Workbook, *Artist's Journal* Magazine

Kingslan & Gibilisco Publications
9851 Louis Drive
Omaha, NE 68114
(402) 397-1239

Jackie Shaw Studio, Inc.
Route 3, P.O. Box 155
Smithsburg, MD 21783

North Light Book Club
1507 Dana Avenue
Cincinnati, OH 45207
(513) 531-8250

Resources

Brushes and Specialty Tools

The Bag Lady
P.O. Box 531
West Stockbridge, MA 01266
(800) 248-LADY/(800)248-5239

Dick Blick Fine Art Co.
P.O. Box 1267
Galesburg, IL 61401
(800) 447-8192

Bette Byrd Brushes
10090 Groomsbridge Road
Alpharetta, GA 30202
(770) 623-3452

CraftCo Industries, Inc.
410 Wentworth Street North
Hamilton, Ontario, Canada L8L5W3
(800) 661-0010
www.craftco.com

Sam Flax, Inc.
39 West Nineteenth Street
New York, NY 10011
(212) 620-3010

Florida Sponge & Chamois, Inc.
2495 Long Beach Road
Oceanside, NY 11572
(516) 678-5600

Grumbacher
100 North Street
Bloomsbury, NJ 08804
(908) 479-4124

Look-Rite Faux Products
1020 B Sterling Avenue
Independence, MO 64054
(816) 833-3719

Michaels Arts and Crafts
8000 Bent Branch Drive
Irving, TX 75063
(214) 409-1300
www.michaels.com

Pearl Paint
308 Canal Street
New York, NY 10013
(800) 221-6845

Plaid Enterprises, Inc.
P.O. Box 7600
Norcross, GA 30091
(770) 923-8200
www.plaidonline.com

Prager Brush Company, Inc.
730 Echo Street NW

Atlanta, GA 30318
(440) 875-9292

ProFaux Workshops & Tool Co.
1367 Girard Street
Akron, OH 44301
(330) 773-1983

Royal Brush Manufacturing, Inc.
6949 Kennedy Avenue
Hammond, IN 46323
(219) 845-5666

Silver Brush Limited
P.O. Box 414
Industrial Park #18
Windsor, NJ 08561
(609) 443-4900

Robert Simmons Brushes
℅ Daler-Rowney
2 Corporate Drive

Cranbury, NJ 08512
(212) 675-3136

Sponge-Man Co., Inc.
201 East Woodside
South Bend, IN 46614
(219) 287-0007

Stenciler's Emporium, Inc.
1325 Armstrong Road, Suite 170
Northfield, MN 55057
(800) 229-1760

Symphony Art, Inc.
130 Beckwith Avenue
Paterson, NJ 07503
(201) 278-7200

Winsor & Newton, Inc.
11 Constitution Avenue
Piscataway, NJ 08855
(201) 562-0770

Paint, Varnish and Glaze Manufacturers

Accent Acrylic Paints
100 North Street
Bloomsbury, NJ 08804
(908) 479-4124

Binney and Smith, Inc.
(Liquitex Products)
1100 Church Lane
P.O. Box 431
Easton, PA 18044
(800) 272-2652
www.liquitex.com

Chroma Acrylics, Inc.
205 Bucky Drive
Lititz, PA 17543
(800) 257-8278
www.chroma-inc.com

DecoArt
P.O. Box 386
Stanford, KY 40484
(606) 365-3193
www.decoart.com

Delta Technical Coatings
2550 Pellissier Place

Whittier, CA 90601
(800) 423-4135
www.deltacrafts.com

Engelhard Exceptional Technologies
ProLine Universal Colorants
12874 Bradley Avenue
Sylmar, CA 91342
(818) 367-1821

Evergreen Distributing, Inc.
Polyvine Products
1612 North Tejon Street
Colorado Springs, CO 80907
(719) 389-0839

Faux Effects, Inc.
3435 Aviation Blvd. A4
Vero Beach, FL 32960
(407) 423-9044
www.fauxfx.com

Flecto Company (Varathane Diamond
Coatings)
1000 Forty-fifth Street

Oakland, CA 94608
(800) 635-3286

Flood Company
P.O. Box 399
Hudson, OH 44236
(330) 650-4070

Fuller-O'Brien Corporation
450 East Grand Avenue
South San Francisco, CA 94080
(800) 368-2068

Golden Artists Colors, Inc.
188 Bell Road
New Berlin, NY 13411
(607) 847-6154
salesgac@norwich.net

Johnson Paint Co., Inc.
355 Newbury Street
Boston, MA 02115
(617) 536-4244

J.W. Etc.
2205 First Street, #103
Simi Valley, CA 93065
(805) 526-5066

Martin-Senour Paints
101 Prospect Avenue
Cleveland, OH 44115
(800) 542-8468

McCloskey Varnish Company
7600 State Road
Philadelphia, PA 19136
(800) 345-4530

Benjamin Moore & Co.
51 Chestnut Ridge Road
Montvale, NJ 07645
(800) 344-0400

Pearl Paint Co., Inc.
308 Canal Street
New York, NY 10013
(800) 221-6845

Plaid Enterprises, Inc.
P.O. Box 7600
Norcross, GA 30091
(770) 923-8200
www.plaidonline.com

Pratt & Lambert, Inc.
P.O. Box 22
Buffalo, NY 14240
(716) 873-6000

Sherwin Williams
101 Prospect Avenue
Cleveland, OH 44115
(800) 752-8468

Shiva By Creative Art Products
P.O. Box 129
Knoxville, IL 61448
(309) 342-0179

Symphony Art, Inc.
130 Beckwith Avenue
Paterson, NJ 07503
(201) 278-7200

Synkoloid (Division of Muralo)
400 Colgate Drive SW
Atlanta, GA 30336
(404) 691-9313

Testor Corporation (Visions)
620 Buckbee Street
Rockford, IL 06114
(815) 962-6654

Valspar Corporation
1191 Wheeling Road
Wheeling, IL 60090
(800) 345-4530

XIM Products, Inc.
1169 Bassett Road
Westlake, OH 44145
(216) 871-4737

Wm. Zinsser & Co., Inc.
173 Belmont Drive
Somerset, NJ 08875
(908) 469-8100

Stenciling Supplies

Accent Acrylic Paints
100 North Street
Bloomsbury, NJ 08804
(908) 479-4124

American Home Stencils
P.O. Box 32007
Franklin, WI 53132
(414) 425-5381
stencils

American Traditional Stencils
442 First New Hampshire Turnpike
Northwood, NH 03261
(603) 942-8100
www.Amtrad-stencil.com
stencils, laser cutting, stencil brushes,
cutting tools, paint, books and videos

Andreae Designs
35673 Ashford Drive
Sterling Heights, MI 48321
(810) 826-3404
stencils

Animal Stencils By Karrie Butler
P.O. Box 1207
Hilo, HI 96721
(808) 969-7809
animal stencils, instructional materials

Art-2-Go Stencil Company
7859 Schenck Road
Perry, NY 14530
(716) 237-5330
art2go@ix.netcom.com
stencils, brushes

B&B Etchall Products, Inc.
18700 N. 107th Avenue, #13
Sun City, AZ 85373
(602) 933-2962
etching creams

Back Street
3905 Steve Reynolds Blvd.
Norcross, GA 30093
(770) 381-7373
www.backstreetcrafts.com
designer blocking presses

The Bag Lady
P.O. Box 531
West Stockbridge, MA 01266
(800) 248-LADY/(800)248-5239
brushes, canvas products, books and
videos

BagWorks, Inc.
3301C South Cravens Road
Fort Worth, TX 76119
(817) 446-8080
(800) 365-7423
www.bagworks.com
canvas products

Adele Bishop, Inc.
P.O. Box 3349
Kingston, NC 28502
(919) 527-4186
stencils, paints, brushes, books and
supplies

Blue Ribbon Stencils
26 South Horton Street
Dayton, OH 45403
(937) 254-2319
BRStencils@aol.com
stencils

Stan Brown's Arts & Crafts
13435 NE Whitaker Way
Portland, OR 97230
(800) 547-3351
mail-order supplier of paints, brushes,
painting books and art supplies

Buckingham Stencils, Inc.
1574 Gulf Road, Suite 1107
Point Roberts, WA 98281
(604) 943-2029
stencils, rollers, supply kits, books and
video

Cabin Craft Southwest, Inc.
1500 West Park Way
Euless, TX 76040
(817) 571-3837
mail-order craft supplies

CraftCo Industries, Inc.
410 Wentworth Street North

Hamilton, Ontario, Canada L8L5W3
(800) 661-0010
www.craftco.com
stencils, brushes, bronzing powders,
books and supplies

DecoArt
P.O. Box 386
Stanford, KY 40484
(606) 365-3193
www.decoart.com
stencil cream paints, acrylic paints

DeeSigns
P.O. Box 960
Newnan, GA 30264
(800) STENCIL/(800) 783-6245
(770) 253-6444
stencils

Delta Technical Coatings
2550 Pellissier Place
Whittier, CA 90601
(800) 423-4135
www.deltacrafts.com
stencils, paints, brushes, books and
videos

Designer Stencils
3634 Silverside Road
Wilmington, DE 19810
(800) 822-STEN/(800) 822-7836
stencils, brushes, stencil cutting tools,
paints, floorcloth canvas, books

Dressler Stencil Company
253 SW Forty-first Street
Department AS
Renton, WA 98055
(206) 656-4515
www.dresslerstencils.com
stencils, brushes, newsletter and video
series

Embellishments/The Mad Stencilist
P.O. Box 5497
El Dorado Hills, CA 95762
stencils

Gladys Grace
213 Killingly Road
Pomfret Center, CT 06259
(203) 928-2034
theorem stencils, brushes and fabric
paints

Graphic Art Systems
Grafix Dura-Lar
19499 Miles Road
Cleveland, OH 44128
(216) 581-9050
stencil film (acetate alternative)

Great Wall
6280 Guyson Court
Pleasonton, CA 94588
(510) 462-8844
stencils, brushes

Jean Hansen Publications
308 Pettipaug Road
Westbrook, CT 06498
(860) 399-5216
theorem stencils and supplies, books

Ann Hooe Ltd.
P.O. Box 9, Dept. SS
Winnetka, IL 60093
(847) 446-7749
stencils

Indiana Coated Fabric
(219) 269-1280
cambric cloth

L'n'J Designs
110 W. University Drive
Mesa, AZ 85201
(602) 833-4565
stencils

Lake Arts
5513 Flowery
Branch, GA 30542
(770) 237-2787
cambric cloth, floorcloth canvas

Makin-It, Inc.
1604 Beaver Creek Lane
Snellville, GA 30278
(800) 357-4954 (orders only)
(770) 985-1382
www.craftnet.org
stencils, brushes, books

Manor House Designs
85 Great Lake Drive
Annapolis, MD 21403
(410) 268-9782
stencils, stencil patterns, Mylar, cutting
tools and video

MC Gannon Stencils
2618 Westchester Road
Toledo, OH 43615
(419) 535-1425
stencils

McKibben & Co.
P.O. Box 470
Hampton, FL 32044
(352) 468-1440
stencils

Michaels' Arts and Crafts
8000 Bent Branch Drive
Irving, TX 75063
(214) 409-1300
www.michaels.com
nationwide craft store

Lynda Mills Designs
37 Whitelands
Fakenham, Norfolk, England NR218EW
01328-856363
stencils

Natural Accents/Lynn Brehm Designs
6965 El Camino Road, Suite 105-415
Carlsbad, CA 92009
(760) 744-3986
stencils, brushes, Mylar, instructional
materials

Nutmeg Stencilers
1286 Mountain Road
West Suffield, CT 06093
(860) 668-2703
theorem stencils, books and supplies

PJ's Stenciling Magic
Easy-Cut Plastic
43 Lockrow Blvd.
Albany, NY 12205
(518) 438-8020
stencils, stencil cutting tools, brushes,
faux finishing mitts and stencil plastic

Periwinkle Artist's Stencils
P.O. Box 457
West Kennebunk, ME 04094
(207) 985-8020
stencils

Plaid Enterprises, Inc.
P.O. Box 7600
Norcross, GA 30091

(770) 923-8200
www.plaidonline.com
stencils, brushes, paints, decorator
blocks, books and videos

Royal Design Studio
386 East H Street, Suite 209-188
Chula Vista, CA 91910
(619) 477-3559
stencils, brushes, books and video

Shiva By Creative Art Products
P.O. Box 129
Knoxville, IL 61448
(309) 342-0179
paint sticks, brushes

Robert Simmons Brushes
℅ Daler-Rowney
2 Corporate Drive
Cranbury, NJ 08512
(212) 675-3136
stencil brushes

Sims Collection
24 Tower Crescent
Barrie, Ontario, Canada L4N 2V2
(705) 725-0152
stencils, brushes

StenArt, Inc.
P.O. Box 114
Pitman, NJ 08071
(800) 677-0033
stencils, stenciling sponges, paints

The Stencil Library/The Stencil
Collector
1723 Tilghman Street
Allentown, PA 18104
(610) 433-2105
British stencils (available cut and uncut)

Stenciler's Emporium, Inc.
1325 Armstrong Road, Suite 170
Northfield, MN 55057
(800) 229-1760
wholesale and discount mail-order
stencils and supplies

The Stencilled Garden
1764 West Bullard
Fresno, CA 93711
(209) 449-1764
stencils

Stencils By Nancy
15206 Walters Road
Houston, TX 77068
(281) 893-6187
stencils, newsletter, books and videos

Strathmore Paper Products
2 Gateway Boulevard
East Granby, CT 06026
(860) 844-2400
paper palettes and other paper products

The Testor Corporation (Visions)
620 Buckbee Street
Rockford, IL 61104
(815) 459-0743
airbrush paints and supplies

Timeless Designs
5401 Chinook Drive NE
Tacoma, WA 98422
(253) 952-8415
stencils

Victoria Trent Stencils
19533 First Avenue NW
Seattle, WA 98177
(206) 546-9491
stencils

V & Olga Decorating Co./Stencillusions
159 Beach 123rd Street
Rockway Park, NY 11694
(718) 634-4415
architectural stencils, brushes

Wallprints/Lasting Impressions
39 San Gabriel
Rancho Santa Margarita, CA 92688
(714) 459-0743
stencils

Yowler & Schepps Stencils
3529 Main Street
Conestoga, PA 17516
(717) 872-2820
stencils, paints, stenciling aprons

Internet Sites

Stencil Artisan's League, Inc.
www.sali.org

Society of Decorative Painters
www.decorativepainters.com

American Traditional Stencils
www.amtrad-stencil.com

Dee-Signs
www.deesigns.com

Dressler Stencil Company
www.dresslerstencils.com

Designer Stencils
www.designerstencils.com

Miscellaneous

Dover Publications
31 East Second Street, Dept. 23
Mineola, NY 11501
catalog of books of copyright-free
designs

Artograph
2838 Vicksburg Lane N.
Minneapolis, MN 55447

(612) 533-1112
opaque projectors and stands

Laserworks
800 Church Street
Ripon, WI 54971
(920) 294-6544
(800) 285-6544
laser cutting service

Educational Institutions/ Schools

Decorative Painting Organizations

Association of Crafts & Creative
Industries (ACCI)
P.O. Box 2188
Zanesville, OH 43702-2188
(614) 452-4541
Fax-On-Demand: (614) 452-2552
acci.info@creative-industries.com
www.creative-industries.com/acci

Hobby Industries Association (HIA)
319 E. Fifty-fourth Street
P.O. Box 348
Elmwood Park, NJ 07407
(201) 794-1133

National Decorating Products
Association (NDPA)
1050 North Lindberg Blvd.
St. Louis, MO 63132
(314) 326-2636

Society of Decorative Painters
393 North McLean Blvd.
Wichita, KS 67203
(316) 269-9300
nstdp@aol.com

Stencil Artisan's League, Inc.
P.O. Box 920190
Norcross, GA 30091
(770) 455-7258

Restoration & Renovation
EGI Exhibitions, Inc.
129 Park Street
North Reading, MA 01864
(508) 664-6455
www.egiexhib.com

Schools

Barth's Faux Effects (Barth White)
3520 Coleman Street
North Las Vegas, NV 89030
(702) 631-5959
www.fauxfx.com/barth.html

Beartooth Designs (Candie Duren)
P.O. Box 255
Red Lodge, MT 59068
(406) 446-2008

Adele Bishop Seminars (Diane Lewis)
P.O. Box 3349
Kingston, NC 28501
(800) 334-4186

Country Owl Arts & Crafts Studio
RR3, P.O. Box 3695
Brandon, VT 05733
(802) 247-3847

Custom Accents Art and Design Center
of Roswell
39 Oak Street
Roswell, GA 30075
(770) 518-3325

The Day Studio Workshop, Inc.
(JoAnne Day)
1504 Bryant Street
San Francisco, CA 94103
(415) 626-9300

Decorative Arts Studio (Zilda
McKinstry)
P.O. Box 227
Main Street
Danby, VT 05739
(802) 293-5775

Decorative Finishes Studio (Martin
Allen Hirsch)
1905 Bardstown Road
Louisville, KY 40205
(800) 598-FAUX/(800) 598-3289
www.fauxfinish.com

Faux Effects (Raymond Sandor)
3435 Aviation Blvd., Suite A4
Vero Beach, FL 32960
(407) 778-9044
www.fauxfx.com

Faux Finish & Business Workshops
(Donna Feltman O'Rourke)
3084 Periwinkle Drive
Snellville, GA 30078
(770) 985-2285

The Faux-Meister (Karl-Heinz
Meschbach)
4901 106th Avenue NE
Circle Pines, MN 55014
(612) 785-2533

The Finishing School (Bob Marx)
50 Carnation Avenue, Building 2
Floral Park, NY 11001
(516) 327-4850

Fletcher Farms School for the Arts &
Crafts
RR1, P.O. Box 1041
Ludlow, VT 05149
(802) 228-8770

Christopher Gurshin Workshop
Seminars
P.O. Box 616
Newburyport, MA 01950

Priscella Hauser Seminars
P.O. Box 521013
Tulsa, OK 74152
(918) 743-6072

Midwest School of Decorative Painting
(Judi Alyea)
155 East Lincoln
P.O. Box 1009
Seneca, IL 61360
(815) 357-1233

Miller Wagenaar Workshops (Phoenix
Miller)
346 North Justine
Chicago, IL 60607
(312) 563-9999

Newport School of Decorative Painting
(Mary Lou Smith)
P.O. Box 1275
Newport, RI 02840
(401) 847-0870

Painted Ladies Studio (Reohn
Zeleznik)
7026 Old Katy Road, Suite 113
Houston, TX 77024
(713) 802-9022

PCM Studios (Philip Meyers)
731 Highland Avenue NE, Suite D
Atlanta, GA 30312
(404) 222-0348

Prismatic Painting Studio (Gary Lord
and Dave Schmidt)
935 West Galbraith Road
Cincinnati, OH 45231
(513) 931-5520

ProFaux Workshops (John Catalanotto
& Greg Frohnapfel)
1367 Girard Street
Akron, OH 44301
(800) PRO-FAUX/(800) 776-3289

Ritins Studio, Inc. (Andrejs Ritins)
170 Wicksteed Avenue
Toronto, Ontario, Canada M4G2B6
(602) 482-1276
www.ritins.com

Rocky Mountain Painting
5390 South Cottonwood Lane
Salt Lake City, UT 84117
(800) 527-9284

San Diego School of Stencil Arts
(Melanie Royals)
386 East H Street, Suite 209
Chula Vista, CA 91910
(800) 747-9767

Vandelae Studios, Inc. (Alison Golder
and Nicola Vigini)
3126 Elliott Avenue
Seattle, WA 98121
(206) 282-9888
www.fauxfx.com/vandelae.html

Index